One Through the Heart

One Through the Heart
More tales of Justice and Injustice
A Lawyer's Memoir

Edward Z. Menkin

Copyright © 2020 Edward Z. Menkin
All rights reserved.
ISBN: 9798651131174

DEDICATION

For Laurie

What, art mad? A man may see how this world goes with no eyes. Look with thine ears. See how yon justice rails upon yon simple thief. Hark in thine ear: change places and, handy-dandy, which is the justice, which is the thief?

>Shakespeare, *King Lear*, Act IV, scene vi.

Table of Contents

DEDICATION v
ACKNOWLEDGMENTS ix
PROLOGUE 1
THE WHINE BENEATH HIS WINGS 3
FLOYD: WHEN JUSTICE CHASES ITS OWN TAIL 12
THE LINEUP 31
ADVENTURES IN PERSONAL INJURY & THE LEO FACTOR 37
TOMMY TWO-MOONS & THE DUMBEST THING I'VE EVER DONE 54
IRISH TRUE LOVE IN THE TRUNK OF A CAR 72
DANNY'S GENIUS FAKEOUT DEFENSE AND LOUIE THE FROG 89
OPERATION WEED AND SEED GOES OFF THE RAILS 102
DEATH DUTY 129
"DOES YOUR DOG BITE?" "NO, BUT I DO." 147
ONE THROUGH THE HEART 159
ABOUT THE AUTHOR 200

ACKNOWLEDGMENTS

Some of these stories took place a long time ago and I am grateful to those friends who helped me by refreshing my memory or taking the time to recall events otherwise long forgotten. I am particularly indebted to Jamie Matthews, retired state trooper and town justice, Tim Knauss of the Syracuse Media Group, my long-time friend and colleague Joe Lucchesi, Congressman Peter King, and the staff of the Onondaga Historical Society for their helpfulness and I sincerely thank them all. I also wish to thank my friends Bill Sheldon and the Hon. John J. Brunetti for their help in proofreading this manuscript.

And as always, my deepest indebtedness is to my friend, guru, former teacher, and keen-eyed editor Bob Gates without whom I never could have brought this book to fruition. I will ever be grateful for his friendship, judgment, and support and for his tolerance in my insisting that punctuation belongs outside of quotation marks.

PROLOGUE

All stories here are true. I have tried to be faithful to events as they actually happened and I have tried, where appropriate, to be mindful of people's privacy, even when their stories were mostly if not entirely public.

Many people who know me or know of me have asked why I haven't written about some of the more high profile criminal trials I have been associated with, particularly homicide cases (Dr. Robert Neulander and Ronald Meadow, each convicted of killing their wives; Mad Dog Allen, convicted of beating his girlfriend to death, abducting their 5 year old son, and then killing him too; Stephen VanderSluys, convicted of murdering several of his children for insurance money). I understand people's interest in these awful events and their curiosity about how I saw and experienced them. But, to be candid, it is simply too painful for me to recount these tragedies and too painful, at least for now, to relive the experience of investing so much of my emotional life into defending these clients. I recognize that that was the mission, that was what I was supposed to do. But not for now. Maybe some other time. I trust that each of the tales I do recount in this book will suffice to give readers some idea of what it's really like to be a part of our justice system. I have loved every minute of it and still believe it's the most important thing I've ever done. And besides, it has been great great fun.

THE WHINE BENEATH HIS WINGS

Problems great and small. That's pretty much the triage that passes for my so-called career these days. I have one client in a murder cold case trying to test drive varying explanations of how his DNA was recently discovered under the fingernails of his estranged wife who was strangled 30 years ago. Another guy is complaining to me about his unpleasant 300-pound female supervisor who looks at him crosswise each day. He thinks she's creating a "hostile work environment" because sticking her angry grill in his face every morning makes it impossible for him to do his work. He's sure there's a lawsuit in there. Me? I'm not so sure.

In any case, today my long-time client Reecey B. called me with his contribution to my task basket. Reecey B. is an interesting guy who, I must confess, was the source of one of my finest hours in defending the ramparts of justice many years ago. If for no other reason than loyalty to a guy who gave me a great story, I have always had a very warm spot for Reecey. Today's contribution was a matter of great importance to him. It involved forty-two dollars' worth of underdone chicken wings. But first some history.

This was a long time ago, when a ringing telephone was

actually an opportunity to get and help a client instead of a call from a telemarketer trying to convince me to expand the reach of my Google profile or sign me up for their exclusive referral service for poor souls who have been seriously injured as the result of dog bite encounters.

So the phone rings and on the other end is the incredibly beautiful Donna, a Lebanese dark-eyed siren who efficiently runs a part of the Federal Court Clerk's Office and tolerates men falling all over her, secure in the knowledge that even the most lascivious male lawyer is simply not going to mess with a Federal Judge's deputy clerk. My friend the devastating Donna was calling with a request. It's hard to say no to Donna.

"Eddie, you've gotta help me out here with something."

"Yeah, sure, Donna. What'd you need?"

"Well, there's this defendant, a really unpleasant nasty guy. He's huge and frightening. He's gone through three assigned lawyers and now he's demanding a new one. And he cursed out the Judge this morning. I'm now supposed to see if I can get him somebody else."

"Sounds like a dream case, Donna."

"Yeah, I know, but I gotta do something here. You're really great with people, you can calm this guy down."

Despite the flattery, I lied. "Well, Donna, I'm pretty busy. What's he charged with?"

"It's a drug case. I know you don't like to take drug cases, but it'd really help me out if you took this guy."

Well, I wasn't particularly busy, but my quota of angry people who were dissatisfied and suspicious of getting an assigned attorney (free to them, of course) was way way over quota at the time and, more to the point, I wasn't anxious to get involved in a Federal drug case. This was not any puritanical whim on my part but rather rooted in the following enduring truths: the Feds don't indict marginal drug cases. Once you get past any possible Fourth Amendment issues of unlawful search and seizure, or listening in on what most people would have thought was a private conversation, the rest of the case involves negotiating a deal to reach a humane cap on the number of the remaining years of your client's life to be spent inside an uncomfortable cage. And the cost of that particular achievement is almost always sitting with your client in a closed room with a pair of angry and overworked DEA agents who have a compelling interest in your client snitching out colleagues and friends who may have an awful lot in common with your client, his drug trade, and/or each other, but nothing remotely connected to anything you know about. These stultifying and unproductive chats were not among my aims and objectives when I went to law school and took the bar exam. So, yes, Donna was right, I'm not a big fan of drug cases.

But still, after all, it was the devastating Donna, and she's asking for my help. So I opt for the graceful escape route, "OK, here's what I'll do. I've got some time this afternoon. I'll go over to the jail and take this guy's temperature. No commitments, but I'll talk with him."

"Oh, Eddie, that would be great! Thanks."

So, in obedience to my pledge to Donna, I wander over to the Onondaga County Jail, a somewhat modern facility whose upper reaches resemble – and you've gotta forgive me for this, but it's true since I'm talking architecture not inmates here– the Great Ape House at the Bronx Zoo. Plenty of clean and air-lit space, a wide common area, two tiers of cages, and steel doors which clank open and closed with an authoritative annoyance. I've been in and out of this facility dozens of times and the custody deputies who man each of the 56 cell pods always react with detached amusement when anybody with a tie shows up and all of the residents are milling about the common areas, playing hearts or watching "The View". ("You a lawyer, man? Can I have your card?")

This time, after I ask for the inmate in question, I am directed to 5B, otherwise known as "Punitive Seg". This place was the Corrections Department's version of after school detention except they had plenty of Haldol, tasers, chains, and a rule of silence. No hearts games going, no TVs. I sign in, am wanded, then frisked, and directed to a molded plastic table and chair ensemble. No confidential lawyer conference alcove on this wing. The deputy says to me, "You gonna represent this guy? He's one angry dude. You want me to stay here?" No, thank you deputy.

After a few minutes, the biggest black guy I had ever seen comes trundling out and over to me. He's 6'5, 250, large afro, and in shape. If my ambition was to meet an NFL defensive lineman in person in my lifetime, I could now check off that box. He's wearing an orange jumpsuit and has got the full shackle thing going: leg chains and waist chain with a small lead for handcuffs which stay locked on his wrists even though this is a "professional visit".

He sits down, looks at me, and signals he's ready to listen. He tells me his name is Maurice but he's generally known as Reecey. I explain to Reecey who I am, give him my card, tell him why I'm there (even at this point I'm not so sure) and ask him how he thinks I can help him. To my surprise, he speaks in an even tone and is as straightforward as an army recruiter.

His story is a variant of the "I was just along for the ride" tale of explanation in a drug case involving a vehicle stop; I've heard a variant of this story a couple of dozen times before.

Reecey says two friends invited him to travel to New York City with them. Just for the ride. For five hours. To the East Bronx. Where they made a brief stop, stepped out of the car, and came back with a package. And started back to Syracuse for another five-hour drive. Reecey didn't ever get out of the car until the police stopped them when they were on I-81 about ten miles south of Syracuse. He didn't know what was in the package, didn't inquire, and had nothing to do with whatever the friends were actually doing. He was just along for the ride.

Apparently, invitations of this sort were not all that unusual for a guy who was 6'5", 250 pounds, since if you're heading out to, say, the East Bronx, there's a certain degree of comfort that one feels when you have a friend the size of Reecey sitting in the front seat.

As Reecey is telling me this story, he's smiling. Even in the few minutes we have spent together, there's a certain chemistry evolving here, and he instinctively knows that I know the story is bullshit. He's just trying it out on me.

I ask him why he was dissatisfied with the three lawyers who had previously been assigned to represent him. He says none of them wanted to listen to him and none of them had any interest in even talking about the possibility that the police did not have probable cause to stop the car when it was returning to Syracuse on Route 81. I ask him who the lawyers were. He gives me three names, a trio of all-stars from the Indolent and Incompetent B team. (I didn't tell him that.)

I said that I understood the frustration he was feeling but then asked him why he had cursed out the Judge. "He wasn't listening to me either, man. He didn't give a shit and he stickin' me with these sorry-ass lawyers." I told him it's never a good idea to curse out a Judge. Reecey agreed that it probably wasn't a smart thing to do and that he probably shouldn't have done it. He seemed sorry about it.

Our fifteen-minute get-together having gone reasonably well, I asked Reecey if he wanted me as his lawyer. He did. So I told him I'd get back to him.

Once back in my office, I call Donna to tell her I'll take Reecey's case.

Long pause. I'm expecting a small degree of relief and gratitude. Not.

"Oh, Eddie. I don't know what to do now."

"Why Donna?"

"I went to the Judge and told him I asked you to take the case."

"And?"

"Oh, geez, don't tell him I told you this but he says, 'Eddie Menkin? You gave this guy Eddie Menkin? No way. Not gonna happen. He's not getting Eddie Menkin.' I don't know what to do now."

I told Donna not to worry about it and that I'd go talk to the Judge. Which I did.

Judge D. was a career Assistant United States Attorney before he became a career United States Magistrate Judge. He was unfailingly polite and low key but there was a weariness about him that signaled that over his many years he had seen and heard it all. Which he had. Fortunately for me (and for my new client) he had a quiet sense of humor and when I knocked on his door he immediately smiled in recognition of my mission.

"You wanna represent this guy? He's an asshole. He cursed me out for no reason."

"He was unhappy with who you assigned to his case." Judge D. had been around long enough to know that Reecey had a point on that score.

"They were next up on the rotation. Not my fault. You want this case? You're gonna be sorry."

Well, I did take the case and I wasn't sorry even though after filing the appropriate suppression motion that Reecey wanted, arguing an illegal search and seizure, we lost and Reecey had to plead guilty and receive a pretty hefty sentence (driven in part by his prior felony conviction in State court). It turned out that the DEA had been on to Reecey's two friends for days and they knew that the Bronx trip was not to take in a Yankee game. The stopover for the package had been surveilled and videotaped and even though Reecey had not been on their radar before, they recognized muscle when it showed up and the Title III eavesdropping recording of one of the friends offering Reecey $1,000 to make the round trip pretty much sent Reecey's explanation of "just along for the ride" to the canvas where it wasn't going to get back up.

So even though Reecey had to go to jail, I had gained his respect and a degree of his appreciation for listening to him, actually working hard for him, and not blowing him off. "Success" in a criminal case ultimately only means your client has been treated fairly. It's a bonus when you get a thank you. And he did thank me. After Reecey did his time, he'd periodically call to check in and even referred a client or two my way.

Which brings me back to the forty-two dollars' worth of undercooked chicken wings.

It seems that two bright and ambitious Syracuse University seniors majoring in finance decided to apply their entrepreneurial smarts and a little of their parents' capital to opening their own business. Their intensive market survey and focus groups told them that opening a fast food chicken wing business would be a hot ticket in the University area. Putting quite aside the fact that they did not much know the difference between chicken wings and airplane wings, they foolishly hired a staff of minimum wage student help whose sum total of experience and expertise in this area consisted of their own fondness for chicken wings.

On the third day the business is open they get a sizeable order for delivery. Forty-two dollars' worth of Jalapeno Hot Wings, their opening week special. The call is from Reecey. He and his girlfriend are having friends over for the season premiere of "Real NBA Housewives". The delivery comes promptly and Reecey's girlfriend answers the door, pays and generously tips the kid, and brings the wings to the kitchen. Double Garlic. Not Jalapeno Hot.

Reecey is mad and calls the wing joint. They apologize for the mix-up and promise to send over a replacement order. Which they do. But now it's three dozen Curry BBQ wings. Now Reecey is ballistic. He's already missed the television program and he's not having any of this. So he takes the wings and drives down to the store himself and starts in complaining the same way he did when he was in front of Judge D. so many years before. Having a 6'5", 250 lb. angry African American guy yelling at you tends to get your attention and these fast order kids go lickety split to their fryer and bing bam boom Reecey's Jalapeno Hots are delivered to him. He leaves, still angry. He gets home, opens the box of wings and finds they are underdone.

So now Reecey is asking me if he's got a case here and if he can sue the wing business. I say to him "Seriously? This is why you're calling me?" He says yeah. I tell him no way. He laughs and says yeah, he thought so.

Then he says, "I got a speeding ticket in Virginia, can you help me out with that?"

Some clients are for life.

FLOYD: WHEN JUSTICE CHASES ITS OWN TAIL

There was no getting around it. Floyd was a bad guy. He was drawn to criminality like a moth to a flame. He began as a minor menace to society and kept working out what seemed to be his career plan in small stages, buffing up his rap sheet here and there so that he could eventually claim to be a big time criminal. He wound up as a guy you wouldn't trust to date your daughter or live next door.

When he was sixteen, Floyd got arrested for possession of burglar tools. Lots of people walk around with a screwdriver, but the plastic slimjim and lock pic key set in his pocket caught the cops' attention, especially since Floyd was leaning against the door of a Chevelle that wasn't his at 10:30 at night. That misdemeanor charge somehow floated away but it was followed about a year later by charges of possession of stolen property and assault. Still relatively minor transgressions, but enough to earn Floyd a six month stay in the County jail.

Not satisfied with these small time blemishes on his jacket, Floyd graduated to strong arm robbery and then residential burglary (fix in your mind for one minute this guy prowling your living room with a flashlight at two o'clock in the morning), achievements which had tagged him with two separate felony convictions and a cumulative 4½ years in State prison by age 22. By the time I got the lucky assignment to represent him on his latest felony charge he was 26, had been previously arrested 11 times, and was on parole (which meant no matter how his latest caper turned out, he still owed the State some time on the old burglary charge).

Floyd was very happy that he got me as his assigned lawyer. My legend, even then, was on the ascendancy, especially throughout the cellblocks in the Justice Center. Most of the inmates firmly believed that if you were interviewed on television you must be a great lawyer. (I had been getting a fair amount of TV time. Reporters like lawyers who can coherently string two complete sentences together when speaking into a microphone.) Truth to tell, there was less enthusiasm on my part, but a court assignment was a court assignment and I never entertained the notion that I wouldn't/couldn't give Floyd's case my best efforts.

Floyd was charged with felony purse snatching from an elderly woman, one of the lowliest crimes you could think of. Coming up with a defense was going to be a challenge, not just because it was really offensive conduct but mainly because the proof against him was pretty strong. Criminal defense attorneys usually have a nearly inexhaustible supply of excuses, mitigations, explanations, or workarounds to make out some kind of defense to whatever criminal charge may be brought against their clients. All those rationalizations stem from the fundamental assumption that the client really isn't all that bad or his conduct in this case was aberrational or excusable. No sale here. There was the faintest of a whisper of a possible defense (misidentification), but Floyd was guilty as charged; he knew it, I knew it.

My demands for discovery from the prosecution were promptly met and that information only served to darken the horizon. I was really stumped. So I resorted to one of the more desperate gambits in my defense satchel by proposing to the D.A. that we could all save some valuable trial time for other more serious matters by letting Floyd plead guilty to two misdemeanors and receive two consecutive one year sentences. Sticking Floyd in jail for two years instead of the fifteen he would face upon conviction for this offense – and as offenses go this one was pretty offensive – didn't appeal very much to the D.A., so my proposal went nowhere. The D.A.'s position was "plea or try" and since Floyd was a predicate felon, a conviction meant some serious time. Plus what he owed to parole. Floyd thought he had nothing to lose by taking the case to trial. So off to trial we went.

The Two Mrs. B's

Mildred Brown was having a nice morning. For one thing, the weather was good and that gave her the chance to roll her car windows down as she was driving her friend Fran to Bob's True Value Hardware Store so Frannie could get some light bulbs. At 81, Mrs. Brown was proud of the fact that she could still drive, and she was enjoying her quiet retirement from being a courtroom bailiff. The job was never very much of a challenge, but, still, she enjoyed wearing a uniform and got to meet all kinds of people. On occasion she would have to retrieve a box of tissues to help console a sobbing witness, but that is about as close as she ever got to the world of true crime. She was a lovely lady and everyone liked her.

On this particular morning, Mrs. Brown pulled into the

parking lot in front of the store. It wasn't so much a parking lot as it was two angled areas of blacktopped sidewalks converging at the corner. Since the store was on the corner of a busy intersection, customers had to park on either the west side or the north side of the building. You really couldn't see what was happening on the other side of the parking area once you chose your spot, but the entire parking area was in wide and plain view from every angle if you were stopped at the intersection of South Salina Street and Seneca Turnpike.

Fran got out of the car and went into the store. Mrs. B. sat quietly behind the wheel listening to the radio. She put her purse on the passenger seat where Frannie had been sitting. Suddenly, but quietly, a dark-skinned African American guy about 6' tall, wearing a white baseball cap, blue jeans, and a light blue shirt, appears at the passenger's side, opens the door, reaches in, grabs Mrs. B's pocketbook and starts to remove it. Startled but not incapacitated, Mrs. B. reaches for the pocketbook, gets one of the handles to tug on, but she is clearly overmatched and the purse snatcher now has the bag and is running away, east on Seneca Turnpike. Mrs. B. gets out of her car and starts yelling but the miscreant is swiftly receding from her view and chasing him would be futile. He gets in a large white Chrysler with rust spots along the bottom and a gold colored roof, and peels off, going east on East Seneca Turnpike. There's a towel covering the car's license plate except for the first letter, which is a J.

Now, you may be thinking that as nasty little crimes go this purse snatch was somewhat thought out and boldly executed. The purse snatcher is bigger, stronger, and 50 years younger than the victim, all favoring a quick grab and getaway. Another smooth move is the covered license plate.

Without those vital digits and letters, who could possibly track down a late model white Chrysler with rust spots along the bottom and having a gold colored roof? Driven by a black man wearing a white baseball cap, blue jeans, and a blue shirt? I mean, what are the odds? But like all crimes of this level and type, the execution has left a few things wanting. Like the facts that a) it is in broad daylight; b) in the middle of a very busy intersection; and c) the victim got up close and personal with the purse snatcher, got a good look at him, and can identify him (and the car).

And then there was the Mrs. Carmen Bradshaw factor.

Prosecutors and police officers often dream of getting a witness like Carmen Bradshaw. At least once a year, they recite the following prayer: "Please, God, send me a witness to a serious crime who is clear-eyed and clear-headed, who saw everything that needed to be seen, and is not afraid to say so in a straightforward way. And please make them someone without a criminal record."

If you are in the criminal justice business long enough, you eventually run into an eyewitness like Carmen Bradshaw. Smart, right place, right time, unobstructed view of the event, not bashful about getting involved, and unshakeable in her determination to see to it that justice is done. If the D.A. could keep Carmen Bradshaw and witnesses like her permanently on their payroll or in their inventory, they would never lose a case.

And so it was Floyd's misfortune that while Mrs. Brown is frantically struggling to regain her purse from the black guy who snatched it from her, Mrs. Carmen Bradshaw is twenty yards away at the wheel of a car stopped for the light at the intersection of South Salina and Seneca Turnpike. Hers is the first car at the light, maybe 50 feet from the Bob's True Value parking lot and she sees everything that was happening.

Hot Pursuit

Incensed by the brazen thuggery unfolding before her very eyes, Mrs. Carmen Bradshaw resolves to run this miscreant to ground. So when the black guy with the white baseball cap and blue shirt holding Mrs. Brown's snatched purse gets into the white Chrysler with rust spots on the bottom and the gold colored roof on top and peels out of the parking lot, Carmen Bradshaw decides to "hit it", and she now winds up in hot vigilante pursuit of the guy, the car, and the purse.

She really guns it and gets right behind the white Chrysler with the still covered license plate. The Chrysler steps on it too, heading east up the Seneca Turnpike hill. The chase is on. The guy immediately senses he's being followed so he engages in evasive action, the main part of which is to careen into and through the warren of small streets, some of which are cul de sacs, which branch off Seneca Turnpike.

Mrs. Bradshaw is not familiar with these streets so she momentarily loses sight of the white car. But she's determined to follow no matter where they are headed. She wishes she had a roof bar of emergency lights to activate, just like the real police have, but since she's without that kind of equipment, she activates her emergency flashers while going 45 mph down what is otherwise a nest of quiet city side streets. She catches sight of the car but he's now in her rearview mirror, going in the opposite direction. She hastily does a U-turn, peels out after him, and is now a block behind him; but she's gaining. The Chrysler speeds up and so does Carmen. They travel about a half a mile through heavy traffic on Salina Street but then the white Chrysler cuts into a shopping plaza. It's full of cars. Carmen loses him in the crowded parking lot.

Both pumped and breathless, Carmen looks around, frustrated and disappointed. She decides to go back to the scene of the crime, Bob's True Value, so she can report to the police who she assumes are already dusting for prints, photographing every angle, and sending a search helicopter up to look for the white Chrysler with the gold top and rust spots on the bottom. In a sulk, she slowly turns out of the shopping plaza parking lot. As she turns onto Salina Street, there's an abandoned donut shop to her left and from behind it emerges the Chrysler. It pulls up right alongside her. Behind the wheel is the guy she thinks she saw snatch Mrs. Brown's purse. It's Floyd.

Both cars stop at the light. Floyd rolls his window down and says to her "Why are you following me?"

Carmen shouts at him, "You stole that old lady's purse!"

Floyd says, "I don't have no purse." He opens the passenger door so she can look in. He says, "You crazy, lady." He shuts the door and drives off.

Floyd partially opening the door to his car is a sobering moment for Carmen B., causing her to rethink her initial exuberance in getting involved in the first place. She is secretly relieved that Floyd drives off. She is subdued, but still determined to right this wrong, and as Floyd drives off, she notices that the rear license plate is now uncovered and she memorizes it: JDT 6501.

Now, these events transpired back in the day—way back in the day—when people didn't have cell phones. Least of all Carmen B. (It's somewhat frightening to conjure up what would have happened had she had one: careening down side streets narrating her frantic pursuit to the 911 operator.) So, Carmen pulls into a tire store, asks to use the phone, and does her Good Samaritan duty by calling the police. By happenstance, there's a Syracuse Police patrol car parked right in front of the tire store (in her frenzied excitement to rush in to make a phone call, Carmen B. didn't see it.). Once she realizes that help is right there, she relates all she saw to the officer, describes the event, the dude who snatched Mrs. Brown's purse, the white Chrysler with the rust spots on the bottom and the gold roof on top, and the car's license plate number. He asks her if she can come down to the police station to give a full statement, but Carmen B. has had enough excitement for the morning, and she realizes she's now very very late for her dental appointment. So she gives him her contact information and leaves the tire store (secretly relieved that she's had enough cops and robbers excitement for the morning).

The cop at the tire store, Henry Burns, III, calls it in.

Back at the Bob's True Value, the scene is not exactly swarming with cop cars and SWAT teams, but an officer did respond and he's interviewing Mrs. Brown. The call from Officer Burns at the tire store comes in and although it doesn't exactly result in a South Side dragnet, it does alert the eyes and ears of other officers and in pretty short order the SPD has located a white Chrysler with rust spots on the bottom and a gold roof on top and a NY registration JDT 6501 parked on Bridget Circle. It's not far from Bob's True Value. It's Floyd's address and Floyd happens to be right there, wearing a white baseball cap, blue jeans, and a blue shirt. He's denying up and down that he had anything to do with the purse snatch and claiming that he had been at work for Advanced Piping at a construction job all morning (doesn't take great police effort to reveal this to be a lie). Floyd very much resembles the guy who grabbed Mrs. Brown's purse. Officer Burns pulls up with a partner. They both realize that the car and the physical description of the perp match a recent "grab 'n go" in the parking lot of Wegman's, so they take the lead in questioning Floyd. Mrs. Brown is brought to the scene and she seals the deal. Yes, that's the car; yes, Floyd's the guy.

This was pretty swift police work. The receipt for Frannie's light bulbs at Bob's True Value is time stamped 11:17. Mrs. Brown's call to the SPD is 11:19. Carmen Bradshaw's breathless account to Officer Burns is at 11:20. Floyd is placed under arrest by Officer Burns at 11:45.

A Trial Going Nowhere

If you are thinking that the case against Floyd is pretty solid, you win the refrigerator, a new dinette set, and the trip to Hawaii. As I occasionally have to remind my clients, I am a lawyer, not a magician. Not only am I out of magic, but Floyd is a predicate felon (this will be his third trip to felony land) and he is eligible for a very very long sentence. In fact, if he is found to be what the law calls a "persistent felony offender", he could technically be looking at a life sentence. But, hey, let's not get carried away here. Though a persistent felony offender sentence is technically possible (I share this data point with Floyd who is sobered by the thought), it's not really likely. Despite his bad bandido history, Floyd is relatively small potatoes. Instead of life, a good solid fifteen years in the clink would probably suffice. (This reassurance didn't exactly brighten Floyd's disposition either.) Then there's more bad news for Floyd. Not only has Mildred Brown positively ID'd him and the car but the case is assigned for trial to the Hon. William J. Burke. I have mentioned Judge Burke before and he played a major role in my career as a lawyer. He was about to play a major role in Floyd's life too: Mildred Brown had retired after many years of faithful service as a court attendant. In Judge Burke's court. Could things get darker?

So on the appointed day I show up for trial. I'm acting confident, pretty much for no reason at all except to make Floyd feel better. I have a bunch of files, photos, motions, and reports in my briefcase, but truth to tell, I got nuthin'. People think I'm a pretty good and clever lawyer; I think so too. In Floyd's case, I got nuthin'. And Judge Burke, though usually very even tempered, seems eager to bypass the jury trial part of this procedural and move straight to sentencing.

My adversary is a young Assistant D.A. named Richard Southwick and he's trying his very first felony case. I knew Richard's dad, Morrell Southwick, a lovely man, and Rich inherited his father's gentility and smarts. Rich was a good lawyer then and later developed a very impressive career as an Assistant United States Attorney. But still, this was his first trial.

Although I wasn't present (Rich related this to me well after the trial was over), it seems that he was wheeling his case file cart out of the office on that first day and he encounters Senior Assistant District Attorney John Duncan. John too was a lovely and smart guy whom I had known for quite a while. John knows it's Rich's first felony trial and asks Rich what he's got. Rich says it's a felony purse snatch in front of Burke. John asks who the defense attorney is, and Rich says, "It's Eddie Menkin." John says, "Watch him." Rich says, "Whaddya mean? I shouldn't trust the guy?" and John responds with, "No, no, that's not it; just watch him."

Well, if Rich was watching me, he must have pretty quickly learned that there wasn't much to see. I wasn't exactly letting him roll over us or get away with anything, but there's really not much you can do if you are trying to cross-examine an 81 year old purse snatch victim who is clear-eyed and sure of herself in identifying the client as the perp. And you are asking the questions in front of the judge who recalls her warmly as one of his staff.

Well, the trial, such as it was, was rolling on uneventfully. Rich was doing a workman-like job and I did my best not to resemble a potted plant. Mrs. Brown testified in detail about how she was victimized, and she confidently pointed out Floyd as the guy who victimized her. She identified photos of the white Chrysler with rust spots on the bottom and a gold roof on top and a NY registration JDT 6501 (except all she saw was the "J"; not exactly a fruitful avenue for searing cross-examination or challenge). Officer Burns takes the stand and testifies to his arresting Floyd and how Mrs. Brown identified Floyd at Bridget Circle. (I had previously challenged that ID procedure in a pretrial motion. It's called a "show-up", a one-on-one-is-this-the-guy? procedure which is generally frowned on because of its suggestivity, but it is also thought to promote efficient and fair police work in case the guy in handcuffs being displayed was not the guy). Judge Burke declined to suppress Mrs. Brown's ID.

So now, after a short day, but one which seemed very long to me, we've picked a jury, given opening statements, heard from Mrs. Brown, heard from Officer Burns, and viewed far too many color photographs of the white Chrysler with rust spots on the bottom and a gold roof on top and NY registration JDT 6501. Rich's next witness, Carmen Bradshaw, lives in Seneca County, about 60 miles away, and she couldn't make it in that day, so we break early ('early" in Judge Burke's courtroom is somewhere between 4:30 and 4:45). Floyd goes back to his jail cell (making bail while awaiting trial and having a parole sticker on you at the same time is a nearly unheard-of phenomenon). I go back to my office to prepare for the next day and think the great thoughts that people think lawyers think about whilst their office doors are closed. Nuthin'. I got Nuthin'.

The Second Mrs. B

Looking back now, it occurs to me that Rich could have rested after the day and that he really didn't need to call Carmen Bradshaw. On the other hand, Rich was a belt and suspenders kind of guy and, more to the point, Carmen Bradshaw not only saw the whole thing in real time but could place Floyd behind the wheel of the car. So we are hearing from Carmen. I briefly entertained the notion that I could perhaps portray her as a bit over-eager to get involved and suggest that her Good Samaritan conduct was in reality a form of her skewed sense of being a vigilante avenger and that therefore she was somewhat less reliable as a witness.

But Carmen turned out to be a pleasant lady on the stand, with a subdued affect, and a readiness to be accurate. With no hesitation, and in a business-like manner, she pointed out Floyd, sitting beside me at the defense table, as the guy she saw steal Mrs. Brown's purse and was behind the wheel of the white Chrysler with rust spots on the bottom and a gold roof on top and NY registration JDT 6501.

Judge Burke looks at me and says, "Your witness, Mr. Menkin." He just as easily could have been saying "Where you going with this?"

So I get up on my hind legs, act respectfully, and gingerly examine Mrs. Bradshaw about her state of excitement at the time she claimed to witness all of this, suggesting, in the most respectful way, that this exciting event may have caused her to be somewhat less than accurate in what she says she saw. She's steadfast. I'm going nowhere.

Then I try one of the oldest tropes there is in the defense lawyer's satchel of desperate cross-examination ploys: You live in Seneca County? You grew up in Seneca County? You went to school in Seneca County? Are there many black people in Seneca County? How many black people have you actually met? One of the great thoughts I had had the night before behind my closed office door was that Carmen Bradshaw, being from a very white, very rural community wouldn't really be able to differentiate an African American from an Eskimo (I actually looked up census data; Seneca County had a white population of 32,731; there were 538 black people living there.) Shamefully racist as my approach was ("all blacks look alike" to some people), I did recognize that there was a glint of uncertainty in Carmen's eyes.

I should have left it there. I should have been content to know that I had raised even a whisper of uncertainty in the witness' identification of my black client.

But, no. That's not me. And although in point of fact I was gathering my notes and papers and starting to turn away from the podium, I asked, pretty much as an afterthought,

"By the way, did anyone ever show you a picture of the defendant prior to today?"

She says, "yes."

I ask, "How many pictures?"

She says, "One."

The roof falls in.

Ka-boom!

Although the jury has no idea of the significance of this colloquy, Richard is in the process of having a minor heart attack and Judge Burke is between boiling and ballistic.

I turn to the Judge and tell him, "I'd like to be heard."

Knowing that a significant motion for a mistrial is about to be made, Judge Burke says, "Finish your cross-examination first."

I tell him, "I'm finished. I'd like to be heard."

He sends the jury out. He excuses Carmen Bradshaw and asks her to wait outside.

"What's your Motion, Mr. Menkin?"

My lawyer friends who practice criminal law will almost certainly understand the gravity and consequences of this little episode. For the rest of you, perhaps a brief seminar on identification evidence and procedures might be helpful to get the full import. Eyewitness identification testimony is usually conclusive and devastating with juries; with lawyers and judges, not so much. Many recent studies and a cascade of cases involving eyewitness testimony leading to gross injustices have led courts and most lawyers to be extremely wary of the reliability of this kind of proof. Especially when it involves cross-racial identification. I mentioned earlier that Floyd was subjected to a "show-up", a procedure where the victim, the first Mrs. B, was brought to Bridget Circle and asked to view, one-on-one, Floyd, the suspect already in police custody. I'm not suggesting that the police were unfair or that Mrs. Brown was mistaken, but, this kind of procedure, in the abstract, could easily lead to misidentification. The question ultimately becomes whether, at trial, Mrs. Brown is identifying the perp who committed the crime or the suspect she was shown by the police a half hour later. Most reasonable people would be inclined to identify the guy because the police have him in custody.

The danger of prejudicial misidentification becomes worse, far worse, when the trial witness, in this case the second Mrs. B., Carmen Bradshaw, is shown a single photograph of the defendant prior to the trial and is then asked to identify him when testifying from the witness stand. Like in the show-up (this is called a "photo show-up"), the question is whether the witness is identifying the person she saw committing the crime or the person whose single photograph was shown to her.

There are pretrial procedures designed to guard against these dangers, the most important of which is that the prosecution is obligated to notify the defense, prior to trial, of any pretrial identification procedures (a line-up, a show-up, a photo array). I obviously knew about the show-up on Bridget Circle; I filed a motion to suppress that ID and that was denied. But I didn't know that Floyd's photo had been shown to Carmen Bradshaw prior to trial (my question was simply a shot in the dark). Therefore, I didn't know before I asked the question that we were deprived of the opportunity to at least challenge Carmen Bradshaw's in-court identification. And to really bollix up the situation, Rich didn't know that either because he hadn't spoken with Floyd's parole officer who was the guy who showed the photo to Carmen B.

So, for all those reasons, Burke is now beside himself and he recognizes that his chance to give Floyd the long ride has all but disappeared. He calls us up to the bench and says to Rich, "This lawyer wants a mistrial and I've gotta give him one. How could you have let this happen?" He pauses, and says, before Rich can respond, "Get him his two misdemeanors."

Rich is crestfallen and embarrassed even though he really didn't do anything wrong. He says he's got to confer with his boss, Senior Assistant D.A. Norm Mordue, head of the felony trial unit.

While hardly elated at this turn of events, I know that the Trial Angel of the Inadvertent Question has wrapped her wings around me, and she has gently kissed Floyd on the cheek. I sit down with him, our heads close together, and I quietly tell him we are going to go to Misdemeanor Land if he pleads to the reduced charge. He understands completely. "No fuckin' way. You're the greatest. We kickin' their ass here." If judgment was this guy's strong suit, he wouldn't have been sitting there in the first place with two felonies and 11 prior arrests in his jacket. I explain to Floyd that it's time to get real and as full of adulation of my lawyering skills as he might be, he needs to listen to me and I'm pretty forceful with him. He reluctantly agrees, but he'll only take a single misdemeanor with one year at the County Penitentiary at Jamesville (or, as Floyd put it, and as many of his equally compromised compatriots were wont to put it, "I'll do the bullet at Jimmyville."). I tell him he's pushing it. He frowns.

Rich comes back in the courtroom and beckons me over

to his table. With shoulders slumped and a sad air of defeat, he says, "I talked to Norm. You can have the two misdemeanors."

I felt for Rich. I really did. But whether it was because of an overzealous devotion to my client or some innate streak of cruelty I didn't think I had, I held up one finger and said "One. He'll only plead to one."

Rich didn't get upset or angry. Probably imbued with a final sense of what-the-hell and I've-got-other-cases-to-worry-about, he just shrugs, flicks his hand, and says "OK. One."

We let the court clerk know that we're ready and after a few minutes Judge Burke emerges from his side door chambers and takes the bench.

Ka-boom! Again. The roof falls in.

The Judge has got his game face on. He motions us to approach the bench. I tell him we've reached a deal and the defendant will plead to a misdemeanor. At first, he doesn't say anything. He waits a beat and then says, "Nah, I'm not gonna do this."

I can't believe what I'm hearing.

"I've thought about it more while you guys were making your deal. This guy's not getting a misdemeanor."

"Judge, you told Rich to give the guy a misdemeanor. I had to talk my guy into it."

"Yeah, I know. I've changed my mind."

Judges, like anyone else, can change their minds, but this was really pulling the rug out from under me It turned out that the Judge's change of heart came about as the result of two separate events. The first was that he was genuinely unhappy over how things had played out and that it didn't feel right to him. OK, he's human. I get that.

The second, and far more disturbing, factor was Carmen Bradshaw. The bravado she put on display by chasing Floyd down after the purse snatch was no aberration. She really was a brassy woman and she was nobody's fool. It turned out that she was the wife of a prosecutor in Seneca County (a fact which somehow escaped my notice and pretrial investigation) and as soon as the photo show-up incident came about during her testimony, she knew exactly what was happening and what Judge Burke was being forced to do. So instead of waiting out in the hallway like she was told to do, she talked her way into Judge Burke's chambers and gave him a major piece of her mind. The Judge didn't hide this shocking impropriety from us; he outright told us that she was yelling at him. She actually intimidated him into doing what he wanted to do anyway after thinking about it.

It's my turn to go ballistic. I loved Judge Burke. He was my mentor through the years I was the prosecutor assigned to his court; he always went out of his way to steer me in the right direction; and I knew he had great affection for me. I loved him like a grandfather and in fact two days before he died he did me the great honor of asking me to speak at his funeral. But in this instance I was furious and it took all I had to maintain a respectful tone. I remind him that he will get reversed if he denies a mistrial, that he was the one who gave the green light to the plea deal, that it was on his say so that Rich had to go to his supervisor to ask for permission, and because of him I had to persuade a client to plead guilty to a crime when he didn't want to.

My rant doesn't make Judge Burke feel any better, but he

eventually backs off and we go forward with the plea.

So Floyd pleads guilty to one misdemeanor and he does the bullet at Jimmyville. He asks me if I will represent him at his final parole hearing, but I decline, telling him that I am out of magic juice.

Criminal defense lawyers each have their own definition of what constitutes a "win". An acquittal is a "win", there's no doubt about that. I know many lawyers who think if they beat the top count in the indictment that's a win too even though the client winds up doing twelve years on Count Three. I have other colleagues who regard a mistrial as a win on the theory that the client gets more time to stay out of jail. I don't count Floyd's case as a win. Instead, I think of it as a high speed car race careening around the criminal justice oval when the prosecution's car hit an oil slick and spun out and Floyd and I just happened to get to the finish line first. But there was no trophy.

THE LINEUP

If you watch a lot of television, it's likely that you have seen more police lineups than have actually occurred in the real world. Corporeal lineups have largely fallen out of favor with most prosecutors and police agencies. One reason is the growing distrust of eyewitness identification testimony. (Who can forget the "Seinfeld" episode when Kramer wants to pick up a few bucks by acting as a "filler" in a stationhouse lineup and winds up being identified as the perp?) Another is that they are notoriously difficult to organize. Early in my career as a prosecutor, I had a case involving a grocery store stick-up committed by a six-foot light-skinned African American guy with a short afro. Plenty of inmates in the Justice Center could fit that description and fill in for a lineup. The cashier was pretty confident of his photo i.d. of the guy but the police wanted a lineup. The problem was that the guy had an identical twin brother and there was only one robber. And to compound the problem, the brother was in the store at the time, innocently shopping. So no matter how similar looking the others in the lineup were, we would run the danger of the guy's lawyer demanding a second lineup with the innocent twin in it. Putting both of them in the same lineup was simply unthinkable. How could we possibly do that? I spent an afternoon trying to placate the cops and wound up telling them I'd do it if they came up with a workable solution. We never did hold that lineup.

I did have one notable experience with a lineup which, I firmly believe, successfully vindicated the wrongfully accused. It was in the Justice Court in the Town of Marcellus.

One of the responsibilities of a young D.A. is to appear at town or village courts to deal with the myriad problems of small town justice which show up with incessant regularity (traffic tickets, of course; but also shoplifting, harassment, trespassing, neighbor disputes, etc.) There are over 1300 justice courts throughout the State and each of them requires the presence of a D.A. from time to time. Sometimes you'd have to appear twice a month in some of the busier courts. It's a burden which extends your day and can cause a fair number of missed suppers with your family. On the other hand, it gives you a chance to do some rough justice and meet real people with real problems. It can also provide you with lawyering opportunities which would never come up in County Court. It also, from time to time, can be a lot of laughs.

So on this one occasion, my day in County Court is finished and it's about 6:30 when I drive out to the Village of Marcellus on the western edge of the County. Back then, the Court was situated in a very small clapboard frame bungalow which might have been built around 1920. Today, some of the larger and more affluent communities have rather handsome and well-appointed municipal buildings which house the local courts, but the Town of Marcellus had yet to get the memo.

In this modest setting, all manner of justice got done. The Judge was a hard-working local excavator named Jake

Schneider, a man whose sunburn and rough-hewn hands bespoke what he did with his days: dig ditches. Jake was a sober, low-key guy who was very deferential to whatever the D.A. wanted to do. There was but one exception, and that would be his wife Jean. Jake may have been elected as the Town Judge, but Jean was the "clerk" of the Court and she ran everything. Jean was a very even-tempered woman whose determination to run things was not to be argued with. Everyone knew this. Don't cross Jean. Neither Jake nor Jean were lawyers of course so they looked to the D.A. on questions of law and procedure.

I walk in with an armful of files for the evening's calendar. There are but two rooms to this humble temple of justice; a smallish waiting room no bigger than the one at your dentist's office and, further in, the "courtroom" which consists of a long rectangular oak table and several wooden filing cabinets housing, I suppose, the archived files of this small town court. There are only two chairs: one for Jake, one for Jean. I make my way through the crowded waiting room. It's always crowded; sometimes there are 40 cases waiting—which means around 40 people plus the stray lawyer who may have wandered in. And that's not to mention the occasional cop who's there with a prisoner or to testify in a speeding ticket case. It wasn't unusual to find people lined up and waiting outside on the small front porch.

My arrival signals the start of the festivities. Jean says "Let's call the leash law harassment case first. We ought to get that cleared up before we start tonight's calendar." Leash law harassment? This was some arcane offense that I was clearly unfamiliar with and I look at Jean in genuine puzzlement. She says, "Wait until you hear this."

In walks a slim and fit blonde woman in a jogging outfit and she's got a major mug on. She is obviously the complainant. Behind her is a guy wearing khaki shorts and a t-shirt and he has a permanent smirk on his face. This duo is followed by a big beefy guy who I recognize as the owner of the village hardware store who was also the part-time Animal Control Officer. He's holding a sheaf of papers which I accurately sense is a complaint of some sort. He starts: "Judge, I've got a leash law violation here and this lady is complaining that the defendant's dog set out after her and she says it's not the first time."

"That's right," the blonde in the jogging suit interrupts. "And I'm tired of this shit. It happens all the time."

Jean admonishes her to watch her language.

I turn to the guy in the khaki shorts and, bypassing the Miranda warnings and wanting to get on to what I believe are more serious matters for the night, ask him "What's the story here"

"It's not my dog."

Blonde jogging lady: "Bullshit. He's after me all the time. I run up on Mudhill Road every evening and when I pass this guy's house his dog comes charging after me, barking and nipping."

The khaki shorts guy is still rhythmically shaking his head from side to side. "It's not my dog."

Blonde jogging lady is getting more exorcised: "Bullshit. He's after me all the time. It's his dog. I know this dog. He's a brown and grey German short-haired pointer."

The khaki shorts guy: "Look. I know it's not my dog. For one thing, I always keep him on a leash or he's on a run. There are three other German short-hairs in the neighborhood. They're all from the same litter. It's not my dog."

I turn to blonde jogging lady. "How do you know the German short-hair that's bothering you is his and not one of the other neighborhood dogs?" She says she's positive and she knows the dog.

I decide to expedite the "trial". I turn to khaki shorts guy: "Can you get those other short-hairs in here when I come back in two weeks?" He says it won't be a problem. I turn to the blonde jogging lady and tell her if she can pick out the guy's dog, I'll prosecute the case; if not, I'm going to drop it. She tells me she's positive it's this guy's dog, she's confident she can identify it, and she's satisfied with what I'm proposing.

They all leave and in the back of my mind I'm thinking I've heard the last of this "case", that the khaki shorts guy won't corral all four dogs and bring them in and that the blonde jogging lady will lose interest.

This turns out to be very wrong.

I return to the little Town Court bungalow in two weeks as scheduled. It's a very hot night and since the Court bungalow is not air conditioned, it's not a surprise to me that there's a larger than usual crowd of people waiting outside. What is a surprise—actually more of a shock—is that when I enter the waiting room, there are four German short-haired pointers obediently sitting in a row, each lolling their pink tongues this way and that, panting furiously in the heat of the small room. They are very handsome dogs and surprisingly well behaved. The khaki shorts guy is, of course, there and he is holding the leashes for all four dogs. There's no way to tell which of these dogs is his (I take it as a given that he has only one dog, but I ask him to confirm it anyway, which he does.)

Blonde jogging lady arrives a few minutes later. She's not three feet past the door when she sees all four dogs and stops short. I look at her and ask, "Well?" She says to the khaki shorts guy, "Think you're so clever don't you?" I ask her what she thinks I can do about this "case" and, now angrier than she was two weeks ago, she says "Forget about it. I'll deal with this on my own" and she stalks out.

I'm not so sure I did the right thing here. The "I'll deal with this on my own" was not the kind of remark that was going to endear me to my supervisors if it ever got back to them, and I did briefly worry over whether this small angry lady owned a shotgun. But it was, I think, small town justice at its best. Or maybe its worst.

As I said before, you can learn all sorts of lawyering skills in Justice Court. I had already known that cross-racial identifications weren't terribly dependable. I could now add to the scholarship and wisdom on that arcane subject: cross-species i.d.'s don't work so well either.

ADVENTURES IN PERSONAL INJURY & THE LEO FACTOR

Lawyers get a third. That's the rule. Nobody knows who made up that rule, when it started, or why it's fair. It's just how it is.

1-800-RUHURT

I never set out to be a personal injury lawyer. Criminal law has always been my calling. But p.i. cases came my way as a natural extension of practicing criminal law. People get to know who you are, you build a reputation for competence, and car accident cases, slip and falls, med mal cases, they just sort of find their way to your door. I've made some money practicing personal injury law, sometimes a lot of money, but criminal law is what I do. And with all deference to my friends and colleagues who are in that particular line of work, doing even a complex wrongful death or medical malpractice case is just short of child's play when compared with a serious racketeering case or, perhaps, an arson or murder. And the stakes really can't be even comparable. In one instance you are responsible for preventing your client from losing his liberty and all his fortune while in the other you're working towards increasing the number of zeroes on a check for his pain and suffering. To me, as far as the moral, ethical, and professional challenges go, it's really no contest.

Another difference between practicing criminal law and maintaining a personal injury practice is how the public perceives what you do. It's one thing to be asked repeatedly, "How can you represent criminals?" Yes, it's tiresome but I am comfortable with the answer and I don't mind taking the time to explain the importance – to all of us – of preserving equal justice under the law, of making sure that all people are treated fairly, of not judging people until they've been given a fair chance at defending themselves. If someone thinks that's pretentious, that's on them. But I have a harder time justifying personal injury work (and I've done plenty) that monetizes other people's pain and suffering, especially when we are inundated daily with television advertisements trolling for clients, some of whom may not even realize that they've been harmed. A mass disaster occurs and at warp speed there are 1-800-RUHURT numbers flooding television screens, with mellow-toned spokespersons for personal injury wizards trolling for the injured, the dead, the friends of the dead, the third cousins of the possibly injured. Then it becomes a business with only the patina of a "profession". When it comes to that, generally it's not for me.

There is no more cynical enterprise on earth than trying to put a dollar value on someone's personal injury, their pain and suffering, their grief, their sense of loss. There is an entire subindustry in the insurance business using supercomputers devoted to precisely this calculation, employing algorithms, actuarial tables, charts, graphs, and reports of how much money it took to satisfy somebody else's claim in the past. And don't for a minute think that there isn't a marketplace for these metrics. How much for that hand? Well, is it a right hand or a left hand? Does it belong to a middle-aged white guy with a family of three kids and a six-figure salary or is it "only" an overweight Puerto Rican cleaning lady who is a single mom supporting four children? Same car accident, same injury. Sure, you can make a fair estimate of how much income will be lost in the future. That's the easy part and it's probably a fair way to look at it, or at least one dimension of it. But what about the pain and suffering each of them experienced? You think those demographics don't matter when it comes to deciding how that is valued?

Every personal injury client I've ever had asks the same uncomfortable common-sense question: how much will the insurance company pay me for my injury? I tell them all the same thing: They don't care about you or your suffering. Insurance companies are in one business and one business only: making and keeping money. They only want to know how much it is going to take to make you go away.

Learning the Dollar Value of Pain

I learned the valuable lesson of personal injury economics very early in my career. And it was a lesson that never left me.

I was out of the D.A.'s Office for a few years by then and seemed to be making a go of a solo practice. I had some early successes in criminal cases, both assigned and retained, and people started regarding me as a comer, something which, of course, pleased me immensely because nobody loves me the way I love me. By happenstance or circumstance, I was approached by John DeFrancisco and John Brunetti, two lawyers who were successful, smart, and each as egotistical as me. We decided to join forces and opened up an office called

"DeFrancisco, Menkin, & Brunetti." Although the name seemed to imply that we were a partnership or a law firm, in reality we were just three friends sharing office space and expenses. One ingredient of our success (and we were each successful in our own way) was that all three of us were devoted fans of Mel Brooks' "Blazing Saddles" and could recite the script of every scene practically word for word. In the midst of a serious discussion about some legal problem one of us would be working on, another of us might offer that "My mind is a raging torrent, flooded with rivulets of thought cascading into a waterfall of creative alternatives." Another spontaneous favorite: "Are you chewing gum?"

What was truly remarkable about our association was the natural and warm collegiality we shared, something unexpected given our individual egotistical personalities. It is not an exaggeration to say that in the very long time we were together (Brunetti was in and out of the practice performing stints of public service), we never once had a meaningful disagreement over anything. Not once. We remain close friends to this day although our career paths have diverged. DeFrancisco became a widely respected and long-tenured State Senator and Brunetti recently retired as a very distinguished trial judge. They still, however, know that Mongo is not so much a who as he is a what.

Well, there came a time when Brunetti felt the need to serve the public beyond just being an excellent lawyer in private practice, so he joined the United States Attorney's Office as an Assistant United States Attorney. That, of course, was a full time and important job, one which precluded his representing people in a private practice. But he still had a handful of pending cases which needed to be resolved before he left for Government service. So DeFrancisco and I agreed to divide those cases between us and conclude them on Brunetti's behalf, paying him whatever his fair share of the earned fee would be (if there was a fee at all). As I mentioned earlier, Brunetti was really a brilliant lawyer but he did suffer from at least one glaring deficiency: he wasn't very good at turning down a prospective personal injury client and, in fact, his judgment on what might be a winnable case was, shall we say, open to debate.

And thus it came about that I took over the case of Brunetti's former client, Brenda H.

Brenda H.

Brenda H. was a warm and sweet person, but an ideal personal injury plaintiff she was not. If you went out of your way to invent a sure-fire loser of a personal injury case, Brenda H. v. P.E.A.C.E., Inc. would certainly be your starter kit. First of all, it was a slip and fall case involving a patch of ice. Slip and fall cases are notoriously difficult to succeed at for the plaintiff and if you take a moment to think about it, that's not so hard to understand. Almost everybody has, at some time in their life, slipped and fallen. Maybe if you've lived in Boca Raton your entire life, you've never slipped on ice, but in the Northeast it's a very common occurrence. So, to start with, a jury in Syracuse wouldn't see that event as so unusual. Compounding that, there is virtually no one who slips and falls who doesn't instinctively blame themselves first. Laying blame on someone else, which comes later of course, is substantially counterintuitive, but that is the essence of the plaintiff's claim in these cases. And then you need to address the "failure" of the property owner to maintain their steps, sidewalk, or parking lot by not shoveling or salting; or maybe they did, but inefficiently or carelessly or belatedly. That's a tough negligence argument to make and prove. So establishing liability in these cases is an uphill slog to begin with, and insurance companies, of course, know this.

Then, of course, there's the identity of the defendant. Maybe the plaintiff has an easier go of it if the defendant is a proven slumlord, indifferent to safety and property conditions. Not in Brenda H.'s case; P.E.A.C.E., Inc., was, in fact, not only a not-for-profit entity but a bona fide charity.

Countervailing those liability problems in every case is the nature of the plaintiff's injury. The worse the injury, the more likely the jury will move closer to the plaintiff's side of the courtroom. It's only human nature; people tend to sympathize with someone who's been badly injured, and the gravity of the injury understandably has an impact on the monetary issues of medical expenses (past and future) as well as loss of earnings and earning capacity. Even though Brenda H. was modestly employed as a motel housekeeper (because she also supported three kids, she also received public assistance), her ability to do even that had been severely affected. She had suffered a serious ankle injury, a trimalleolar facture which required the surgical insertion of plates and screws. The x-rays alone bespoke how serious and painful that had to have been. So, notwithstanding that it was a shaky liability case, there was a pretty good reason to press forward and see if we would be able to settle her claim. We demanded $32,000. It was so long ago, I can't remember what our rationale or basis was, but I do remember discussing it with both Brenda and Brunetti. Given all the circumstances, wobbly liability but a serious injury, we thought that the demand was fair and that it would at least generate a reasonable counteroffer.

No dice.

The case was being defended by the prestigious law firm of Hancock & Estabrook and my friend Dan Berman, who was a year or two ahead of me in law school and had had extensive experience defending the interests of insurance companies (which I never held against him), was assigned the file. Dan was a good guy; he liked to smoke cigars while driving his convertible around town in all manner of weather (and Syracuse has weather). Despite his friendliness, he wasn't in the business of just handing over his client's money. Danny told me that the file had been stamped "No Pay" when it arrived on his desk and that he didn't have any authority to settle. On top of that, he was unusually candid with me: "Eddie, look, I don't know why you and Brunetti took this case. Your client is an overweight biracial unmarried mother of three by three different guys and she's racked up $18,000 in medical expenses paid for by the County's Social Services Department. And they've already slapped a lien on the file. And you're suing a charity for Chrissakes. I've got nothin' to offer you and I couldn't pay even if I wanted to. Which I don't."

The "overweight biracial unmarried mother of three by three different guys" part stung, but I couldn't argue with him. Facts are facts. He knew, as I knew, that overweight plaintiffs don't do well with juries in personal injury cases (the insurance companies' algorithms and supercomputers helpfully confirmed what we both knew from experience). But still, the "No Pay" position was both heartless and unreasonable. We weren't going to just fold our tents and leave. A trial was what we were going to have. Or – and most if not all trial lawyers know this – we'll start a trial and see if we could get them to blink.

The Leo Factor

We drew the Hon. Leo F.X. Hayes as our trial judge. Leo was an overweight blue-eyed cherubic faced Irishman, a large man who seemed to have come straight out of the Irish pol playbook. He had a high-pitched and nasal voice which became more high-pitched and more nasal when he became agitated. Which was often. He had an ironic, dry, and bawdy sense of humor except with those lawyers he couldn't stand and to them Leo was not such a fun guy. For them, he had a permanent case of Irish Alzheimer's; you forget everything but the grudges. He was Irish to his core and grew up on Tipperary Hill (where a traffic light emblematic of the neighborhood's deeply Irish character was intentionally installed upside down so that green was always on top). Leo became widely known, and generally well-liked, when he served as the County District Attorney, an office which he deftly parlayed into lots of networked friendships and eventually a seat on the Supreme Court bench (in New York, the court of general trial jurisdiction is called the Supreme Court. It is not "Supreme" but it is the court where most important business gets done). Although he no longer had anything to do with criminal cases, Leo had a special affection for and loyalty to the District Attorney's Office and if you were an alum you started with a leg up with Leo. And I, of course, was an ex-ADA.

Files gathered, trial suits on, witnesses in the hallway, we are ready to go. Danny and I walk into Leo's chambers to discuss what lies ahead. I am hopeful that Leo will squeeze out a settlement here, even something modest we could live with. Without being cynical about it, we all know that Leo F.X. Hayes is not about to devote a couple of precious trial days in the Supreme Court to a piddly-ass slip and fall case. And, beyond that, Leo had a reputation for being able to settle cases.

After initial pleasantries, we get down to business.

"So, Eddie, whaddya got?"

Oh Judge, very bad injury, very sweet plaintiff, struggling to support her three kids. Did I mention very bad injury? Surgery. Plates and screws. She slipped in a parking lot and they hadn't shoveled.

Leo's baby blues are fixing me with just the hint of a twinkle. He's heard versions of this story dozens of times. He doesn't move, he stares, and only says "Uh-huh."

He turns to Dan. "What's your position Danny?"

Oh, Judge. They're suing a charity. They plow the parking lot all the time. She just wasn't watching where she was going. And there's a DSS lien of $18 grand.

"What are you lookin' for, Eddie?" Leo asks.

"$32,000, Judge. There hasn't been an offer."

Leo sits in silence. After 20, 30 seconds of deliberation, he leans forward. "OK, here's what we're gonna do. I'll get DSS to take 6, she'll get 6, the lawyer's gettin' 6." He doesn't discuss this proposition with either of us. He just announces that's how it is and is gonna be. There's really no arguing with Leo and the truth of the matter is that I would almost certainly agree to the $18K and call it a day. We were not, I knew, dealing from a position of strength and $18K was better than nothing and a no cause from the jury.

He doesn't wait for either of us to respond, but turns around and picks up the phone to get the DSS Attorney, Harold Silverman, on the phone. "Harold? it's Leo Hayes. I'm trying to settle a case here." He then pretty much forces Silverman to agree to take $6,000 in satisfaction of the County's $18,000 lien for medical expenses. Satisfied that he's done a good day's work (by now it's 9:45 in the morning), he turns to Dan and says, "Go get me the 18, Danny. Make your call." Dan is about as gobsmacked as I am, but he dutifully gets up and leaves to go call his claims manager.

Leo then turns to me and it's just the two of us in the chambers. "So, how's it goin' Eddie?" He's interested in how all of "his boys" are doing ("his boys" includes former ADA's, even those who didn't work for him back in the day). We wind up gossiping about who's doing what around town, about so-and-so's wife having just left him, and who just got a million-dollar med mal verdict ("that guy's about the worst lawyer I've ever seen.") Twenty minutes goes by. Dan re-enters the room. Leo looks up. "Whaddya got Danny?"

Dan holds up two fingers. "I got two grand. I was lucky to get that out of him."

Upon receiving this news, Leo's cherubic face is suddenly not looking very cherubic. His look has now turned very dark and he goes on for a few minutes about asshole claims managers and lawyers who can't settle cases. He then disgustedly tells us to go pick our jury. We are, after all, now going to have a trial, one in which we all know it will be Danny's turn in the barrel.

Brenda H. v. P.E.A.C.E., Inc.

Most of my trials were me against my opponent or

opponents. The trial of Brenda H. v. P.E.A.C.E., Inc. proved to be a somewhat different affair. It was a triangulated contest with, naturally, me against Danny; but that was only a part of it. It was also Leo against Danny and that, as you might expect, was no contest at all. There wasn't any objection that Dan made that Leo sustained. When Dan asked for a bathroom break, Leo said he'd think about it (he relented after 10 minutes). I naturally was interested in winning, but Leo's "help" was making me uncomfortable. Danny took it like a soldier, mainly because he simply wasn't stupid enough to complain and because he assumed Leo was going to get over it eventually. Which he did.

We spent the morning picking a jury and delivering opening statements. I can't remember very much about what I said except that I emphasized the idea of being a responsible neighbor and that Brenda had suffered a really bad injury because somebody (not exactly sure who) had been negligent. In the afternoon, I called Brenda to the stand and she did a pretty good job describing how she was picking up her kids from day care and then spent the evening in the E.R. with a really gruesome ankle injury. I called the guy who ran the snowplowing service for P.E.A.C.E. and he admitted to missing the plowing, shoveling, and salting that he was supposed to do after a snowstorm hit the night before. I probably asked some questions which called for hearsay answers or which were arguably inadmissible, but Dan's objections fell on Leo's very deaf ears. I offered the deed to the parking lot into evidence to show that P.E.A.C.E., Inc. did in fact own the property. By the end of Day 1, I was entertaining the vague notion that we might actually win, notwithstanding that the law of liability in slip and fall cases was pretty steeply stacked against us. I still wondered why Brunetti had taken this case, but the mission was the mission.

Day 2. I called the surgeon who operated on Brenda and he supplied the jury with a running commentary on Brenda's X-rays (hard to miss those plates and screws) and the rest of her medical records. It cost us a couple of thousand dollars to have the guy take the morning off from his practice and come in to testify and after that money was spent we were all in; no funds left to call her physical therapist or an economist to explain the impact Brenda's injury would have in her life going forward. The last piece of evidence I offered was a certified weather report showing snowfall accumulation and temperature drop in the area (the readings were from the airport). Even though there was a statute that said, specifically, this kind of hearsay evidence is admissible, Dan objected and Leo, having relented somewhat over his anger at Dan's disobedience to his settlement edict, reserved his decision on admitting it. I then rested my case and we took a twenty-minute break.

Despite the beatdown Dan was getting from Leo, he decided not to call any witnesses, confident that our case hadn't met the legal threshold to establish liability. And I was fearing he was right. So we were about to move on to summations when Dan asked to approach the bench.

We are now huddled in the front of the courtroom and the jury is about 15 feet to our right. In a low voice, Dan says to Leo, "Judge, I got the 18."

Leo says, "Great. It took you long enough. We're done here."

He looks over to me and he now sees there is hesitancy in my face.

I tell him, "Judge, I gotta talk to my client first."

Leo, stunned, says, "What?"

"I gotta talk to her."

Leo says (and this was nearly 30 years ago but I can remember it verbatim as if it was yesterday), "Look, Eddie, your case is a piece of shit all right? If your client wasn't such a sad soul I would have no caused you after your opening statement. She's gonna take the $18K, awright? And I'm telling you right now that if this jury comes back for her I'm gonna set it aside."

I say, "Aw Judge."

Leo says, "Don't 'Aw Judge' me. I've wasted enough time on this. Go talk to her."

Leo tells the jury we have a legal matter to discuss and he sends them out.

I sit down with Brenda and start explaining the facts of life. I had told her the day before, of course, that the Judge wanted us to settle for $18,000 but the insurance company had only offered $2,000, so we didn't really have to make any decision at that point. But now, they've stepped up with $18,000, just as the Judge wanted them to, and although our demand had been $32,000 she ought to very seriously consider the offer. I didn't tell her what Leo had just said to me only minutes earlier, but I did tell her that he "strongly" felt we should settle for the $18K.

She says, "Oh, Mr. Menkin, that's really not fair. I have a really bad injury." I couldn't argue with her on the bad injury part; as to the "fair" part, who's to say what's "fair"? She then says, "This jury likes you a lot. I've been watching them and they're really paying attention to everything that you are saying. And they like me. I can tell. When I was testifying they were really paying attention." I tell her it's going to take more than just who the jury likes better, but she's now adamant. She wants to take her chances with the jury. I don't have it in me to tell her of Leo's threat to set aside a verdict in her favor, and somewhere in the deep recesses of my brain I'm trying to rationalize it as just another part of Leo's bluster performance art. So I get up and return to the bench.

"Judge, she won't take it."

He just stares at me, making it clear that I now have switched places with Danny in the barrel.

We step back to our respective tables, the jury is called in, and Leo asks me if I have anything else. I say no but remind him that he hasn't yet ruled on my offering the weather report into evidence. He picks it up from the bench in front of him, looks at it again, and says "Denied." He holds it out towards me and says, "Here, you can take it along with you to Rochester." I doubt that the jury even heard this last part, much less understood it, but Rochester was where the Appellate Division was located and what Leo was telling me once again (not that I needed reminding) was the best I was gonna do was an appeal from him kicking a verdict in our favor if that miracle was ever to occur.

We then launched into our summations, perorations which I am sure were both equally forgettable. I know mine was because the only thing I can and do remember is that with every third word I would glance over at Leo who had the look of a very large bird of prey who was eyeing a much smaller bird caught in a bramble (that would be me).

Leo then instructs the jury on the law of negligence and how it applies to cases of a person injured after slipping and falling on ice. Sometimes a judge will convey, if only by intonation, how the jury might favor one side or the other. Had Danny not shaken loose the $18K from his claims adjuster manager at the last minute, I probably could have gotten some kind of subtle help from Leo when he instructed the jury. No way. In fact, a reasonable person could have taken what Leo said as a suggestion that Brenda really should have been more careful. On top of that, he also seemed to go out of his way to emphasize that sympathy should play no part in their deliberations.

The jury retired to deliberate and immediately set about to address the first important item on their agenda: ordering lunch. Notwithstanding it would take some time for the tunas on rye and the BLTs to get delivered, and the jury would then probably want to eat before even beginning to deliberate, I decided not to return to my office which was 6 blocks away but rather just hang around in the courthouse with Brenda. This proved to be a mistake. Brenda's optimism, her faith in the kindheartedness of the jury, her unwavering support of me, and her repeating over and over what a great job I had done, were almost painful to listen to. I had been distracted during my summation by Leo's dire warning and that sense of uneasiness didn't leave me at all while I sat on the oak bench outside the courtroom listening to Brenda. I'm fearful and conflicted over whether I should tell her what the Judge had said he would do if we got a verdict in our favor. It was as if we were traveling down a pretty country lane on a sunshiny day and Brenda was my bunny rabbit companion who didn't know there was a giant reticulated python down around the next curve in the lane. Maybe the most merciful thing would be for the jury to decide against us and then we'd be done with it, a really awful thought, one which made me feel even worse for thinking it.

The awful moment arrived much earlier than I had expected. At least there was a small mercy in knowing that this was going to be over quickly. A note came out. The jury had reached a verdict. This is always a bowel-churning moment, one that is stressful beyond description in a criminal case for sure, but even in a civil matter like this one, it creates real anxiety.

The little ritual always plays itself out with clocklike regularity, no matter what the stakes are. The parties assemble, the judge takes the bench, the jury comes in and the foreperson hands the verdict sheet to the court clerk who hands it to the judge. The judge then reviews it, hands it back to the clerk who then hands it back to the foreperson who reads it aloud.

Verdict: P.E.A.C.E., Inc. was negligent.

Verdict: Brenda was not negligent.

Verdict: Damages awarded to the Plaintiff in the amount of $47,000.

Brenda is beside herself with joy and gratitude, quietly weeping. She hugs me. I stand up, thank the jury, thank the Judge, and do my best to just get out of Dodge.

Dan is too much of a gentleman to make his motion to set aside the verdict right then and there so he asks the Judge for a date when he can file his post-trial motions. Leo gives him a date, thanks the jury, gets up from the bench and disappears behind the judicial curtain.

I'm not sure of what I want to do other than to get the hell out of the courthouse. I gather my files, my briefcase, my coat, and Brenda and we head for the door. The courtroom is on the third floor; Leo's chambers are on the fourth and he's standing by the elevator about 15 feet from the courtroom and he's directly in our path. I opt for the down stairway just a little further away. Brenda has my arm and she's still bubbling with gratitude as we pass behind Leo. As we go by him, he doesn't turn, but says, "Nice job, Eddie." I get out a "Thank you, Judge," just as the elevator doors open and Leo steps in.

He turns and looks at me directly. The doors to the elevator are closing and Leo says, "You're gonna be all right kid."

And I was.

TOMMY TWO-MOONS &
THE DUMBEST THING I'VE EVER DONE

This is a story about pretty much the stupidest thing I've ever done. I can't believe that I'm actually writing this down because apart from the handful of people who were involved, very few people have ever heard about it. At least I hope that's the case. I know I've gone out of my way not to tell people about it. But still, it's worth telling. And it's worth telling for a couple of reasons. It's worth it to me to remind myself at least occasionally that I'm really not quite the great smart lawyer I like people to think I am. But there's a more important reason to tell it. It's a useful reminder (one that younger attorneys would do well to heed) that if you are a defense lawyer who treats the cops with respect and an understanding of their job, there may come a time when they will do you a solid if you really need one. And on this occasion, I needed help. In a major way.

Akwesasne

This twisted little saga had its start on the Akwesasne Reservation, a good-sized swath of land (about 35 square miles) that is mostly in Canada but straddles the St. Lawrence River and extends into New York State (the New York portion is called the St. Regis Mohawk Reservation). The Mohawks settled the land about 250 years ago and they consider it sovereign territory. It's not Canada, it's not the United States; it's Akwesasne. Despite the powerlessness that most Native American tribes have experienced in our country, there is a pretty fierce sense of independence among the 12,000 or so people who live there. Their sense of independence notwithstanding, they are plagued by the same social ills that torment many Native American communities: poverty, alcoholism, and unemployment. Smuggling is a long tradition, with marijuana, cigarettes, and people being the commodities of choice. It's not a major shock to discover that there are a lot of guns there.

Tommy Two Guns

Living on the Rez was a young guy named Tommy Two Moons, a beefy pony-tailed Mohawk from the St. Regis. He was periodically employed as an itinerant carpenter and laborer, traveling from construction site to construction site and picking up work where he could. His father, grandfather, and two uncles all worked the high steel in constructing the skyscrapers of New York City, a long and prideful tradition for the Mohawks, who prized bravery and were not afraid of great heights. But technology and the use of giant automated cranes largely eliminated the need for these Native steelworkers and their exploits faded into legend.

Tommy supplemented his income by working as an occasional courier for one of two rather large-scale marijuana smuggling operations, each run by a different faction. Although they pretty much dealt with the same product, because they had the same source of supply, the Bucktooth

Crew was in an uneasy competition with the Jacobs Posse. But since Tommy was trusted and dependable, and was related by blood to members of each crew, he didn't have any trouble making the occasional run for one or the other. He really wasn't a player in either organization, just an occasional helper working his network of stops. Like a bread route delivery guy, picking up cash here, delivering kilos of high quality weed there. He drove an old beat up Cadillac with a large trunk where he stored his carpentry tools. Plenty of room for contraband. And for a good long while he appeared to be nothing other than an overweight Indian looking for work, driving an old car which was just a couple of miles short of junker status.

On this one occasion, Tommy was asked to make a 10-kilo weed delivery to a guy in Watertown, a two-hour ride from the St. Regis. He was given two large sturdy nylon gym bags. One was maroon and contained the 10-kilo load. The other, beat up and blue, held a very different kind of package, something that made Tommy more than a little nervous: two AR-15s, a sawed-off shotgun, and a MAC-10 machine pistol. He was supposed to drop off the guns to a couple of Bucktooth guys at a location on the southern edge of the reservation, but when he got to the meetup spot they weren't around. Not wanting to be late for his Watertown run, and definitely not wanting to drive across the "border" into the town of Bombay, which was in New York State, he found a place to stash the guns and decided to go on his way to Watertown with just the weed. He figured he'd hook up with the Bucktooth guys later that night. That never happened.

Tommy's drive to Watertown was uneventful. Back on the St. Regis, though, things were getting busy in a hurry. Just as

Tommy had begun his drive, the Feds swooped in on a long-planned raid, scooping up most of the Bucktooth crew, including the two guys who Tommy was supposed to deliver the guns to. Their absence from the meetup spot for the guns was attributable to their sitting in the back of a DEA van, wearing zip-tie handcuffs and sour expressions. As he drove south, Tommy knew nothing of what was going on. The Federal raid had garnered some very serious weight, mostly marijuana and some fentanyl, but the expected cache of weaponry came up a little light. Through their informant, the Feds had expected to recover at least two AR-15s, a sawed-off shotgun, and a MAC-10 machine pistol. The guns didn't materialize and the only guys in the Bucktooth Crew who thought they knew the location of the guns weren't in much of a disclosure mode. In fact, only a few knew that they had been given to Tommy to transport and no one other than Tommy knew their present location. So the Feds had to be temporarily content to have a bunch of drug-dealing Indians in cuffs and a substantial amount of drugs on the table.

Unaware of this turn of events, Tommy drove on to Watertown. His knowledge base expanded rapidly, however, when he showed up at the designated spot to find not only the 10-kilo customer waiting but also a small group of DEA agents who took possession of the kilos, the customer, and Tommy. Of course, they didn't know anything about the extra drop Tommy was supposed to have made with the guns, and Tommy decided his best course was just to go along with the program, submit to arrest, keep his mouth shut, and get a lawyer. That lawyer turned out to be me.

Tommy got arraigned in Federal court and got detained without bail. I met with him in the Justice Center after receiving the assignment to represent him from the Federal Court Magistrate Judge. When meeting with your assigned client for the first time, especially if the meeting is in jail, as this one was, trust building is really the first—and only—order of business. Finding common ground with the client is usually a reliable avenue into a productive dialogue. Could be anything from pro football to mutual acquaintances to cooking. It really doesn't matter. I have found that most people talk to me fairly easily (I have inherited my beloved and colorful father's habit and ability to be able to talk to strangers with little hesitancy). Although certainly not sullen, Tommy didn't open up to me at all. He wasn't unfriendly, he just didn't tell me very much. As I came to learn, part of his success in evading trouble and doing his occasional courier thing was his inclination to mind his own business and keep his mouth shut. But he was clearly interested in what was going to happen to him and what the possible sentence could be. I told him that being behind the wheel of a big-ass Cadillac with 10 kilos of weed in a gym bag in the trunk didn't bode well for him.

He didn't, at this first meeting, tell me anything about the blue gym bag. On the upside, because his drug running was only an occasional gig and his inclination was to keep to himself, he really didn't show much of a profile that got the Feds' major interest. From what they knew—and their information was accurate—he was not much more than a peripheral player, if a player at all. Still, there was that troubling gym bag. The maroon one with the drugs. Our first meeting didn't result in much more than my telling him what the charges were (he didn't need a refresher on the available evidence; the gym bag was the gym bag). He did disclose to me that his brother Reggie lived on the Onondaga Indian Reservation right outside Syracuse and he asked me to call Reggie and get him to visit him in jail.

I reached out to the U.S. Attorney's Office where I was pleased to learn that Tommy Two Guns was not much more than an afterthought, a runner who didn't show up very much or very often in their DEA-6 reports. He may have had some exposure to a conspiracy count (substantially jacking his sentencing range well beyond the 5 years max he could get for just the 10 kg load in his trunk) but I didn't detect any strong interest from the Government in leaning on him. I left the meeting without any commitment from them (I didn't expect one), but I had a sense that a modest sentence wouldn't be an unreachable objective.

Reggie

I called Reggie. My intention was just to convey Tommy's desire for a jail visit, but it turned out that Reggie was deeply concerned about his little brother's dilemma and he was eager to meet with me. This was more than okay with me, particularly because I wasn't getting much feedback from Tommy and, in keeping with my usual M.O., I really wanted to learn a good deal more about my client and his story.

I hit it off with Reggie right away. He was a big, handsome, well-built guy who wore his long black hair in a ponytail. He had played professional lacrosse for a time (lacrosse has near religious meaning for the Mohawks and Onondagas) and he was now employed by a tree cutting service, a job that suited his athleticism, strength, and agility. Reggie knew a lot about the Bucktooth and Jacobs marijuana operations but had steered clear of them and criminality in general. He had already researched and asked around about me and was satisfied that I knew my way around Federal court. He asked a lot of questions about sentencing guidelines (there were many) and the prospects of suppressing the 10-kg of marijuana in the maroon gym bag in the trunk of Tommy's Cadillac (there were none).

Reggie had just come from his jail visit with Tommy. Not surprisingly, he had acquired a whole lot more information about his brother's activities than I had been able to gather. Reggie was astute enough to realize that the case against Tommy was pretty strong, at least insofar as possession of the marijuana went, and that the only sensible approach to lessening his potential punishment was cooperating with the Government. But only up to a point. To Reggie, and to Tommy, providing information about any of the individuals in the Bucktooth Crew was unthinkable. It just wasn't going to happen. Reggie wasn't a lawyer, of course, but he didn't need to be to understand that a deal was in Tommy's best interest. Since a deal—any deal—consisted of one side giving the other something they wanted in exchange for something you wanted, Reggie took a creative approach to Tommy's problem. "Information"/testimony from Tommy was out of the question—but Reggie knew that there was something else of value we could offer. It was at this point that he told me about the blue gym bag and the guns.

This of course got my full attention.

Guns were like a magic elixir with the Feds. They were like Reggie Jackson's self-described role on the New York Yankees: the straw that stirs the drink. For the Feds, a marijuana bust, even a big one, was just another day at the office. Guns in the hands of criminals on the other hand, particularly of the AR-15 variety, could get their attention in a hurry. And if you could lead them to a cache of weaponry in the hands of the bad guys, you scored extra stars on your report card.

I had had a pretty warm relationship with two ATF agents, Harry Maxwell and Tony Stewart, and even though the Bucktooth caper was a DEA case I still thought that our best avenue to the bonus round of cooperation for Tommy was through the ATF if we could find a way to put the guns in the Government's hands without anyone else getting hurt. So I reached out to Harry and engaged in a little chumming, sprinkling what I thought would be some attractive bait over Federal waters looking to see if I could stir up some interest on the Sea of Cooperation. I intimated to Harry that I could put him on to the "missing" guns. This got Harry's interest, but he made it clear that he was in no position to give me any guarantees. Although he didn't sound dubious, he was careful not to sound too eager either (but he knew and I knew that he was definitely eager). I was purposely vague enough to get him to understand that I wasn't in any position to deliver yet. Just sayin'. I told him that I would have to work on it.

It wasn't more than 45 minutes later that I got a call from the DEA. The Bucktooth raid was their caper and the agent knew full well about the guns that had come up missing. I was noncommittal with him too and told him what I had told Harry: I was working on it. It was clear that my chumming was paying off.

It was at this point that I formulated what turned out to be the stupidest move of my career. I would take possession of the guns, hold them for a short while, nail down a commitment from the Government that Tommy would get a significant benefit, and then deliver the guns to the DEA or the ATF. Genius. What could possibly go wrong?

A Great Idea is Born: The Case of Anthony B

The germ of this plan probably grew out of a somewhat similar experience I had had a few years before this and that had had sort of a happy ending. I was representing a young guy named Anthony B., a quiet and very large kid who played tackle for Nottingham High School. Anthony was somehow persuaded to act as muscle in a planned drug rip-off, the targeted victim being a guy who owed Anthony's two companions both drugs and money. The trio drive out to Camillus, a middle-class whitish suburb where three black guys in a car would be, if not a novelty, surely something that would be noticed. They bring along handguns (Anthony didn't have one, so one of his companions helpfully gave him a large and rather clunky revolver.) The robbery gets off to an uneasy start when they break into the dealer's apartment to find the guy in bed with his girlfriend; she is terrorized and immediately starts crying. Things go downhill from there. After seeing the guns, the dealer tells his erstwhile robbers that his money is in a safe back in Syracuse and they have to go back there to get it so he can pay what he owes them.

They all wind up in a car heading back to Syracuse. The girlfriend is still so spooked by the guns that she starts caterwauling, and she's sticking her head out the window, screaming she's being kidnapped. This gets the attention of a lady walking her dog, then the 911 operator, then the Camillus P.D., and finally the Sheriff's Department. There's a chase. It ends up in the large parking lot of an apartment complex near a middle school and in short order sleepy

Camillus goes all Baghdad. Shots are fired and Anthony, big as he is, is scared shitless and runs off into the woods behind the apartment complex. He never fired the revolver (probably didn't know how) and he ditches it in some nearby bushes along a path between the parking lot and the school. The police chase Anthony down two blocks away, put him in cuffs, and take him to the Justice Center where I meet up with him later that night. (His mother called me).

Anthony is very forthcoming about the story and gives me all the details. He is very sorry. He is on schedule to get a lot sorrier if the cops don't recover the gun. They know he had to have ditched it, but don't know where. I am horrified to learn that the loaded gun is in some bushes next to a school. Anthony draws me a map (I am startled by his artistry because it is a very clear map) and he sketches out for me where the gun is. Since I don't have an investigator on my payroll and I am confident I can locate the gun by myself, I drive out to Camillus, find the parking lot, the path, the bushes, and then the gun. At this point, prudence and common sense take control of my brain and I do what I should have done in the first place: I leave the gun where it is, contact the D.A., and get an agreement that if we produce the gun, Anthony won't be charged with possessing it (a concession of minor dimension since he was looking at Robbery 1, but a concession nonetheless). I accompany an investigator from the D.A.'s Office back to Camillus and he retrieves the weapon.

The Plan

If you have been following this meandering side trip through the Camillus Adventures of Anthony B. and The

Gun in the Bushes, you will have recognized the crude exoskeletal outline of the plan I was formulating to help out Tommy Two Moons. Missing gun(s). Nobody else knows where it is/they are. Get the guns to the po-lice. Things go a little easier on my client.

I decided I'd follow the same playbook. Sort of. There was just one teensy-weensy variation. Instead of bringing the ATF to the guns, the genius buccaneer in me decided it would be sort of an adventure in macho-cool and self-sufficient boldness if I got the guns myself and delivered them to the ATF. This was nothing less than a pitiful combination of hubris and execrable judgment, a recipe for disaster, as you shall soon find out.

I ran the plan by Tommy Two Moons at the jail before doing anything. As far as he was concerned, if Reggie thought it was a good idea Tommy was OK with it. It was pretty obvious that he trusted Reggie; me not so much.

The Drop

I once again call Reggie. We agree to meet the next afternoon on a side road on the Onondaga Indian Reservation where Reggie will have the guns to transfer to me. I find the unpaved road pretty easily (the Reservation is not that big) and Reggie is there with the blue nylon gym bag. He opens the trunk of his car, opens the bag, and shows me the guns. I take the bag (it was much heavier than I expected), put it in the trunk of my car, and drive off. There was no conversation at all. There didn't need to be. I just left.

By now it was around 6:30 in the evening and I drove straight to the State Tower Building where I maintained a suite of tastefully decorated offices which bespoke something between ostentation and opulence and consisted of far more space than I needed (intentionally designed to impress clients with what a big deal I was). I had been paying such excessive rent for these offices that the building manager let me use an equally large but dusty and vacant office suite right next door at no additional charge. I had used a couple of the rooms to store a variety of cabinets, files, and enlarged exhibits from past trials. As far as I knew I had the only key to this makeshift storeroom (besides, of course, the building's cleaning crew which occasionally stored unused furniture from other offices there). I thought it would be the perfect place to stash the guns for a few days, giving me enough time to square things up with the Federales.

I laid the bag down in the far corner of a small rear room, right next to a stack of banker's boxes of closed files. I unzipped the bag one more time and felt an almost juvenile titillation when I stared down at the small collection of bad guy guns: two AR-15s, a sawed-off shotgun, and a MAC-10 machine pistol. At that point in my life I had neither fired nor even held a gun of any kind, so I have to admit that just looking at them gave me a small case of the wobblies. I locked the door and went home.

I'm Too Smart by Half

The next day, I start dialing for dollars. I called Harry at ATF and then I called the U.S. Attorney, telling them I could deliver the small cache of bad guy guns they had been looking for. Thinking I was a really shrewd deal maker, I succeeded in getting an oral commitment that putting the guns in the Feds' hands would result in the hoped-for reward for Tommy: substantial cooperation which would lessen his sentence. We agreed I'd get the guns to them the next day. (I just wanted a bit more time to explain this again to Tommy Two Moons).

It's now around 2:00 P.M. For a reason I really cannot explain, I decide to go next door to the vacant office set of storerooms to check on the guns.

They are not there.

Panic is too modest a description of what I'm feeling. This is somewhere between heart-attack-nausea and deep-seated terror. I can barely stand. There is no question that the guns are missing, and they almost certainly have been stolen within the past 24 hours. Literally no one other than Reggie knew that I had them and even he did not know where I had secreted them.

I go back next door to my office and spend several minutes simply composing myself. The thought of calling Harry at the ATF or the U.S. Attorney and telling them "Never mind" was too humiliating to even contemplate. Even worse—much worse—was thinking about my obligation to go over to the jail and tell Tommy Two Moons what his supposedly competent lawyer had just done.

In desperation, and because it was the only remotely logical thing I could think to do, I call the Criminal Investigation Division of the Syracuse Police Department to report that my office had been burglarized. I get a lieutenant named Stevenson on the phone. Although I knew a ton of cops, I didn't know him at all. Somehow that made it easier for me to report to him what had happened. (Not the entire humiliating story, of course, just that I was holding on to gun evidence in my storeroom and it had been stolen overnight.) Maybe it was a slow afternoon for CID, maybe it was because it was the mildly amusing (amusing to them) story of a victimized lawyer, or maybe it was because I used the magic shazam word—guns, but whatever the reason, Lt. Stevenson said he'd send somebody right over. Which he did.

A Visitor from the East

Two cops showed up, Steve Stonecypher and Mark Abraham. I knew each of them in passing, but it turned out that Abraham knew a lot more about me than I knew about him. He was a tall and well- built Palestinian, probably the only true Arab on the Syracuse Police force. He had a myriad of connections in the Palestinian community in Syracuse, a larger group of people than you might expect, and those relationships served him, and the SPD, well. He knew a lot of people. Apparently, I had very favorably impressed him with my work several years before as a Special Prosecutor in a difficult and circumstantial homicide case involving the murder of a Palestinian woman. Her grieving family traveled from Israel to Syracuse to attend the trial and we became very close. My wife and I hosted them at our home to ease their comfort, and our relationship with them became more widely known within the local Palestinian community than we understood or appreciated.

I related the gist of my dilemma to the investigators (leaving out Reggie on the back road on the Onondaga Reservation and how I came to recover the guns in the first place; no need to really complicate things beyond the obvious embarrassment). Stonecypher listened silently, giving a look that this reported burglary was just another call, just another day at the office. Abraham, on the other hand, seemed to be listening particularly closely, giving me a smile which was both empathetic and puzzling to me. I almost thought that he might have been finding this story of a foolish lawyer taking chances with guns as mildly amusing. But that was not it at all.

I was truly unaware that he had held me in fairly high esteem because of my past help to the Palestinian family from Israel and that he really did want to help me. It was more than that though, but once again I was unaware of it. He was smiling because even as he sat there, he had not only formulated a good sense of who would have committed this gun burglary (the State Tower cleaning crew were obvious suspects) but he also knew that he had a very reliable informant out on the street and that if there were guns like these suddenly on the loose this guy would know about it pronto.

The cops left after a twenty-minute visit. Painful as that was, what I really dreaded was breaking the news to Tommy Two Moons. For maybe two, three nanoseconds, I considered not telling him at all. Since that was out of the question, I engaged in a torturous little exercise in weighing how long to delay telling him could be ethically justifiable. That too led to a no-brainer. I had to let the client know immediately. So, with a trepidation I hadn't experienced since I got up to recite the haftorah at my bar mitzvah, off I trundled to the Justice Center, got in to see Tommy, and broke the news of what a reckless fool I had been. True to form, Tommy didn't show much of a reaction. He just stared at me. I told him, unconvincingly, that this would work out. I left for home where I could throw up in the privacy of my own bathroom.

Whatever Laurie made for dinner that night, I can assure you I didn't eat it. She knew something was wrong, but I selfishly declined to let her inside my tale of hubris and humiliation. I was very tired and decided to go to bed, but that too was a futile exercise since sleep was out of the question.

Salvation

Around 10:30 P.M., the phone rang.

It was Investigator Mark Abraham. He had recovered the guns. I was so relieved I didn't bother to ask him how he made that happen, but there was little question that his informant had worked some snitch magic for him. Abraham confirmed all this for me many months later, but to this day I really have no clue about how this undoubtedly interesting back story developed. I was overwhelmed with gratitude and tried to express that, but Abraham just laughed and said he was happy to have helped. The guns, of course, weren't going to come back to me; they found a home in the SPD property room where Abraham logged them in as "recovered contraband." They eventually found their way over to the ATF and I assume were then melted down in the same pyre that was used to consume confiscated firearms and lawyer egos.

Although thoroughly drained by the emotional tumult of the day, I still felt the need to let tell Tommy Two Moons the "good news". What was "good' about it was largely a matter of perspective. For me, of course, the recovery of the guns and my indescribable relief was about the best thing that could have happened. For Tommy, however, it could easily be seen as his reckless and incompetent lawyer desperately involving the police in a situation he might have preferred to remain quiet. I once again drove down to the Justice Center.

It was now after 11:30 and although I had been to the jail many many times before, this time and at this hour it seemed ominous, cavernous, and quietly imposing. I took advantage of the rule which allows lawyers access to their clients 24/7 and found my way up to the pod on 3B where Tommy was housed. Apart from the deputies at the lobby's security desk, there was no one around and the eerie silence extended into the pod where, of course, all the prisoners were locked in and presumably asleep. The one deputy at the pod control desk seemed surprised to see me but he didn't question my need to see my client, even at that hour. He buzzed Tommy's cell to unlock the door. It took a while until Tommy Two Moons stumbled out of his cell, bleary-eyed and seemingly out of it. It only took a minute or two for me to tell him of the guns' recovery; I had no plans for an extended conversation. My hope was that Tommy would show relief and gratitude. But just as before, Tommy gave me little or no reaction other than staring at me and then grunting, "Yeah, that's good. I gotta go back to sleep." Maybe the guy was so used to things going wrong for him that his default reaction to all things was quiet acceptance.

The End (sort of)

Things worked out pretty well for Tommy. And for me too, I guess. Most of the Bucktooth Crew got sentences which ranged between 3 and 6 years. Tommy wound up with 16 months in the slam. All things considered, it was on the light side and the judge specifically credited him with the "voluntary surrender of firearms". The judge didn't know any of the back story of the lost and found guns and that was perfectly fine with me. The "happy ending" for me here is that, apart from the very few players involved, very few people ever found out how foolish and reckless I had been.

From how I've recounted this tale, you may have concluded, as I did, that Tommy Two Moons was a quiet Native American construction worker who was not much more than a low-profile courier who found himself over his head by getting involved in a large-scale drug smuggling conspiracy. That was pretty much my impression at the time and the one I succeeded in selling to the Government. But if this story hasn't already convinced you of my lack of judgment, consider this: 10 years later, Tommy Two Moons was arrested at the Canadian border with $235,000 in cash secreted in various parts of his truck. It wasn't somebody else's money; it was his. He confessed to the DEA that he and his brother-in-law had been running their own operation for years, smuggling high grade marijuana from a Hell's Angels outfit out of Montreal, regularly moving loads of 250 pounds and more. He told the DEA, "I'm known for weight".

This time, Reggie didn't call me for legal assistance. And neither did Tommy.

IRISH TRUE LOVE
IN THE TRUNK OF A CAR

When I was growing up in the 1950s in the Bronx, I thought the world was Jewish. Everybody I knew, everyone my parents knew, almost all my neighbors, they were all Jewish. We lived on the southern border of a Jewish neighborhood and the line of demarcation was just about a block away on West 190th Street, a heavily Irish block. In fact, the Irish, very few of whom were Jewish of course, inhabited a large area across University Avenue and extending south to Fordham Road. I can't say if it was my innate timidity or my fear of strangers which warned me to avoid the area. But I have a clear recollection of being afraid of the Irish Catholic kids who, in my imagination, were just down the block and around the corner lurking and banding together, armed with primitive sticks and anti-Semitic taunts to jump upon my brother and me should we foolishly venture into their territory.

But that was then and I'm glad to report I eventually got past my apprehensions about the Irish. One of my happiest memories as a graduate student was knocking about Dublin and the surrounding countryside and meeting the warmest and most convivial people I had ever known. And, of course, you can't practice law in my community very long without meeting and bonding with smart, tough, and funny Irish lawyers and judges.

So, while I have to confess that the St. Patrick's Day Parade was never a big deal to me (its principal function being to provide an opportunity for daylong drinking and fighting), early in my solo legal career I got to get up close and personal with a side of Irish culture which I had never had occasion to think much about: that would be Sinn Fein, the I.R.A., and a brand of mayhem which was quaintly known as "The Troubles."

This was some time in the summer of 1985. I got a call from the Federal Court Clerk asking me to come over for an arraignment at 2:00. P. M. because Magistrate Judge Ed Conan had assigned me to represent a young guy named Gerry Doherty. I told the Clerk that I was in the middle of a really busy morning, that I was just starting a deposition in an important case in a few minutes, and then I had to head over to the D.A.'s Office for a discovery conference in an arson case. Couldn't she assign someone else? "No," she said, "Judge Conan specifically said he wanted you. Please be here by 2:00 P.M."

The Clerk wasn't particularly forthcoming with details except for saying it was an "interesting" immigration case. As I grew older and more experienced, I came to learn this to be a warning signal since "interesting" cases frequently came packaged with sharp thorns and leaves of poison sumac. But Judge Conan was a really fine man, benevolent and witty, and I instinctively knew he wouldn't be sending me something toxic. And, by the way, he was Irish.

My usual practice was to meet with my client as soon as I

could. I can't recall very many times when I didn't follow this practice. But in this case I had a handful of immediately pressing obligations that prevented me from finding out anything about this Gerry Doherty guy or the charges against him. So I had to settle for just showing up in the courtroom to meet him face to face for the first time. It's actually amazing to me how many lawyers opt for this method of initially meeting with a client; it happens far more than people think. "Hey Mr. Defendant, I don't know you, you don't know me, I don't have a clue as to what your case is about, but I'm gonna be your lawyer. You got nuthin' to worry about."

When Irish Eyes Aren't Smiling

Judge Conan's courtroom was a small narrow room with counsel tables placed very close to the judge's bench. There was a set of three blonde wooden rows in the rear, which constituted the public gallery. As I came down the hallway to the courtroom, I saw a small clutch of people milling about at the entrance. As I got closer, I realized that they were not "milling about" but rather were impatiently clustered at the doorway, frustrated by the fact that the public gallery seats were full and the court bailiff wasn't letting anyone else in.

The bailiff recognized me and let me into the packed courtroom. Seated at the defense counsel table, wearing jailhouse greens and a set of handcuffs, was my new client, the said Gerry Doherty. Seated next to him, also in greens and cuffs, was a petite, pretty, auburn-haired, middle-aged woman who I later learned was named Maire Dolan, Gerry's co-defendant. On the table in front of them was a set of papers which constituted the Complaint: felony conspiracy to obtain illegal entry into the United States. Maire Dolan was a United States citizen (she started out life as Mary but as her allegiance to Eire grew, she became Maire); Gerry was definitely not. They had been arrested at the U.S.-Canadian border when Gerry was discovered hiding in the trunk of Maire's car. How he came to be there would turn out to be a very long story.

I was stunned by the number of people who had wedged themselves into the small courtroom, not just because there were a lot of them but because it was only the night before that Gerry and Maire had been grabbed at the Ogdensburg, New York border crossing. Gerry was from Belfast, Maire from New York City; they were hardly locals who had family or acquaintances in Syracuse. So how did so many people show up on such short notice? And, more to the point, why?

I only had a few minutes to introduce myself to Gerry. He was 26, a good looking medium sized guy with blondish brown curly hair, a very thick Northern Irish accent, and an easy manner. He seemed immediately comfortable with me and not particularly stressed out over his predicament of having been arrested and finding himself in a United States Federal Courtroom. As I came to learn, this custodial experience was on a par with a vacation in the Bahamas for Gerry, since he had recently spent about seven years in Long Kesh prison, a notorious facility in County Maze, just south of Belfast which had gained international notoriety for its harsh conditions imprisoning terrorist convicts from the I.R.A. And how Gerry got there?; well that too was a long story.

But we didn't have time then for long stories.

Gerry introduced me to Maire, who was sitting to his

right. She smiled but we had no chance to exchange peasantries (if that's the right word for this circumstance) because the bailiff called out "All rise!" and Judge Conan hobbled into the courtroom using his cane and took the bench. Judge Conan was a very kind man and the fact that he suffered from rheumatoid arthritis didn't dim his positive outlook on life or on the people who appeared before him. He didn't seem bothered, or even surprised, by the crowded gallery.

Judge Conan was unfailingly polite with everyone and expected precision in the proceedings. He moved immediately into addressing both defendants, telling them that they had been charged with felonies punishable by up to 5 years, that they had a right to a lawyer, that they had a right to remain silent, and that they had a right to be heard on the issue of being released on bail. At the mention of "bail", there was a stirring in the gallery that became an angry murmur when the prosecutor, Assistant United States Attorney Bill Pease, said that the Government opposed any bail for Gerry Doherty.

Judge Conan then asked Maire if she wanted him to assign her a lawyer. She responded that she was going to retain her own counsel but that he was from New York City and would be in Syracuse the next day. The Probation Department had already provided Judge Conan with enough information about Maire (U.S. citizen, lived on Long Island, no previous criminal record) that he was inclined to release her on bail. The prosecutor didn't object, so Maire was ordered released.

With that, Judge Conan decided to adjourn the matter for two days and set a date and time for a bail hearing for Gerry, who would remain in custody. The whole proceeding didn't take more than 15 minutes. Maire was let out of her handcuffs and was embraced warmly by the people in the gallery. I told Gerry I would meet up with him at the jail later in the day.

When the Marshals moved to escort Gerry out of the courtroom there was a brief moment of tension when the gallery started to surge around them and call out words of support and encouragement. The Marshals got him out of the courtroom pretty quickly.

Judge Conan had left the bench, his courtroom deputy was quietly shuffling papers, and Assistant United States Attorney Bill Pease had wisely opted to slide out with the Marshals, so it was just me left in the courtroom with 30 or 40 strangers, all of whom were looking to me with some fairly palpable suspicion. It didn't take long for me to understand that they knew what was going on. Or at least what they thought was going on. I had been appointed by the Judge (a.k.a. The Government); I didn't look Irish (perceptive lot). They seemed dubious; they just wanted to know if I was a guy who could become a believer.

A thin, pale, heavily freckled guy with a cascade of unruly butterscotch hair and wearing a rumpled short sleeved shirt stepped forward and introduced himself. I caught the "Sean" part of his name, but he spoke so quickly and had such a heavy brogue I couldn't catch the rest of it. He was joined pretty quickly by another clutch of equally Irish-looking people, and they explained to me that they were all from the Fulton, New York chapter of NORAID, otherwise known as Irish Northern Aid. As I came to learn, NORAID was also otherwise known to the United States Government as a not so benign group of citizens who rather openly raised funds for Sinn Fein and the IRA. And these weren't cookie sales; according to the Government, the IRA used these funds to acquire guns and explosives training, even though NORAID had protested for years that all they were doing was supporting legitimate political protest in Northern Ireland.

So, they wanted to know what did I know about The Troubles? Had I ever been to Ireland? What did I know about NORAID? It didn't take me very long to come to understand that my interest was Gerry Doherty, but their interest was the idea of Gerry Doherty. Not exactly adverse interests, but from the get-go I was leery of them and they weren't full-on embracing me either.

One of the ladies gave me a slip of paper with her name and telephone number, and told me to call should Gerry Doherty need anything. I assured her I would. She also gave me some literature about NORAID. She said the group "had to check some things out" (presumably about me) but that they would return for the bail hearing in two days. I thanked her, and the others, for their support. But in truth, I had no clue what was going on with these people, and I quickly excused myself to get over to see Gerry Doherty. And that turned out to be a memorable interview.

Gerry Doherty's Story

By the time I made it over to the Public Safety Building Jail, the local media was all over the story of this "interesting" immigration case. This was a time when Syracuse still had an afternoon paper, and even before I got to the PSB entrance I was taken aback by the headline blaring from the sidewalk news box: CONVICTED IRA TERRORIST BOMBER NABBED AT THE BORDER. Yeah, I thought, Gerry and I had a lot to talk about.

Gerry turned out to be a quietly charming guy and the story he told me seemed to have more than just the patina of truth. Even though this was early in my career, my bullshit detector had already been tuned and adjusted to a high performance level and Gerry didn't move the needle much past zero during the couple of hours we spent together.

I'll skip the "he grew up in a poor section of town" part of his personal history (there was no "poor section" because everywhere in Belfast was poor), but suffice to say that being Catholic and being a politically conscious young man in Belfast in the 1970's would test any young person's sense of social commitment. Dodging plastic bullets by the time you were nine years old did not do a lot to enhance your sense of security. His peers in America may have left Max Yasgur's farm in Woodstock fueled by a social consciousness joyfully supplemented by LSD and marijuana, but Gerry and his companions were surrounded daily by stark social, political, and religious differences which were dangerously amplified by violence, pistols, and car bombs. Sinn Fein and the IRA were everywhere and you either stepped up or stepped off. The British considered the IRA terrorists, and the residents of Belfast – irrespective of their political leanings – saw the British paramilitaries in the same cruel and terroristic light. And they were mostly scared shitless of the IRA too. Suffice to say, this was a brutal place to grow up.

Beset by wave upon wave of violent sectarian insurrection, euphemistically referred to as "The Troubles", Belfast was nothing short of a war zone. "Trouble" came to Gerry Doherty in a major way when he was just 18. A bomb destroyed a car dealership and the police rounded up "the usual suspects", Gerry amongst them. Although he claimed that he was not directly involved (he knew a guy who knew a guy), he was brutalized into giving what passed for a confession and was summarily tried, convicted, and imprisoned in the notorious H-Block of Long Kesh prison for 8 years. Widely known and condemned by Amnesty International as a concentration camp, with its ongoing prisoner protests and hunger strikes, Long Kesh outdid even Angola for its inhumane conditions, and it gained international notoriety for its suppression of political prisoners. Many prisoners adopted extreme methods of protest: prolonged hunger strikes, refusal to use toilets or showers, refusal to wear prison uniforms and donning soiled blankets instead (it was called "going on the blanket"). Gerry participated in these protests at the H-Block of Long Kesh. He spent 8 years of his young adult life there. (His sentence was actually for 12 years but he was released early.)

During his incarceration Gerry engaged in a correspondence relationship with Maire Dolan in the United States. I never learned how it started, but the little I did know led me to believe that Maire was deeply committed politically to the IRA cause and chose to reach out to a young man she regarded as a political prisoner. Over the course of years their letter writing became more personal, and by the time Gerry was released they had resolved to marry.

Maire traveled to Ireland and then accompanied Gerry to the United States Embassy in London where they naively sought to obtain a visa for Gerry to enter the United States. Their intention was to get married in New York where Maire's aged parents lived. She said it was important that her parents meet her fiancé. As they should have expected, the

U.S. Embassy was not enthusiastic about granting permission to a felon convicted of an act of IRA terrorism, particularly a bombing. The application was denied.

Undeterred, Maire and Gerry traveled to Canada, thinking for some reason that obtaining an entry visa into the United States would be easier there. Again, they visited the United States Embassy and again Gerry was denied.

Out of legal options, and thinking that it was imperative that Maire's aged parents get to meet her intended, their next stop was the counter at Avis Rent A Car, making sure to get something with a large trunk. They drove north from Toronto and tried to enter the U.S. at the Ogdensburg, New York. Maire was unable to suppress her nervousness and the border agent who asked her to pull over for an inspection wasn't much of a romantic, even after he heard their story.

This, in sum, is the story Gerry told me. Parts of it were pretty easy to corroborate: the bombing, Gerry's conviction, Long Kesh, the embassy visits. It had the outlines of a story I felt I could sell. If I had to. The part that was a little wobbly for me was Maire's aged parents. How aged and/or infirm would they have to be to stop them from hopping on a Greyhound to Toronto, or Montreal, or even Kingston? Really, I didn't get the urgency. Since Maire had a lawyer, I didn't feel comfortable in just dropping in and asking her. Another part of the story that I thought was in need of a little buffing was why, if they had such an innocent intent, they had to drive more than 200 miles from Toronto north to Ogdensburg to cross over into the U.S. when it was a much shorter ride to Niagara Falls. It would be a lot easier to answer these questions if Gerry was out of jail. We'd have to await the bail hearing.

The Bail Hearing

The bail hearing arrived. If it was at all possible to fit more people into Judge Conan's small courtroom, NORAID was able to do it. It was heartening to Gerry to see this show of support, and I felt perhaps more confident and emboldened than I was entitled to be by their presence.

There are a lot of variations when it comes to the laws relating to bail, but when all is said and done it comes down to two basic questions: 1) is the defendant likely to return to court? and 2) if he is released, does he constitute a danger to the community? There are other factors which are relevant, of course; like what is the strength of the evidence against the defendant? In Gerry Doherty's case, I figured I didn't have much of an argument that the Government didn't have sufficient proof to convict him. What would I argue? That he was a worker at the Avis Rent A Car lot in Toronto, some of his coworkers pranked him by locking him in the trunk of a rental car, and this Maire Dolan lady picked up the car and drove it 233 miles without her knowing he was in the trunk? Not a winning argument.

I thought that the Government, in the person of AUSA Billy Pease, would hammer the "danger to the community" angle because after all Gerry was convicted of an IRA bombing and the newspaper seemed more than comfortable in calling him a "terrorist". On the other hand, given the almost comic circumstances of his entry into the U.S., it wouldn't seem that the plan was for him to get into New York for the purpose of committing mayhem. Nevertheless, Billy went for it.

In response, I gave one of the more operatic arguments I

had in my repertoire, asking rhetorically what "community" Gerry Doherty was actually a "danger" to. Standing between Judge Conan and the army of NORAID supporters seated in the gallery, I asked "Do these people seem fearful of having Gerry Doherty released into their community?" I then got a little carried away and went into a lecture, reminding Judge Conan of the many and deep contributions the Irish had made to our local community: "…in politics, in medicine, our educational system, and the law." Judge Conan's expression didn't change much but his visage and affect pretty clearly was telling me "Calm down, son. I get it."

I really didn't think that "risk of flight" was going to be a significant factor. Obviously, Gerry had no roots or ties to the community and no assets or property he would abandon should he choose to take off. But I still tried to minimize that possible argument by pointing out that it would be logically counterintuitive to fear that Gerry would run away when the essence of the charge against him was that he was trying to get in, not get out of the United States. It really wasn't much of an argument and Judge Conan decided to keep Gerry in jail basically because if he did release him there didn't appear to be any place locally he could go. And he said exactly that.

The bail "hearing" didn't take very long and I was once again face-to-face with a crowd of very Irish looking people, and they weren't very happy. They couldn't understand why Judge Conan declined to set bail for Gerry. They complained that the Judge was "betraying" his homeland. One guy said Judge Conan looked just like one of the ancient "lairds" who suppressed tenant farmers. (In truth, the Judge did have a sort of aristocratic bearing, but it was certainly overridden by his kindly affect.) I told them, particularly the lady who had offered to help Gerry "any way we can", that if we could identify a local family to house and vouch for Gerry, Judge Conan might reconsider. It was a pretty thin hope, but at least it was something. She said she'd look into it and would get back to me. She never did.

They then talked excitedly about the demonstration they were planning in the coming days in support of Gerry and asked me if I thought it would help. I cautiously said yes, but what I was really thinking to ask them was who did they think it was going to help?: Gerry or Irish Northern Aid? I knew full well that the United States Attorney couldn't care less about how many people marched outside the Public Safety Building, waving placards and signs and voicing support for their boy-o. What bothered me even more was that I never heard from the lady who made an offer of help with "whatever Gerry needed."

It was clear to everybody that Judge Conan had left open the possibility that he would release Gerry on bail to a responsible local person with ties to the community; nobody from NORAID stepped up. It became clear to me over the weeks I worked on the case that it wasn't so much that Gerry Doherty was important to them; it was how he was emblematic of The Troubles that got them pumped. It wasn't that they didn't care about him. They just cared more about The Cause, and the longer that Gerry was in the slam the easier it would be to parade around with placards and give speeches and draw attention to the injustices infecting Belfast.

Thanks for visiting

I gave it a few days and then made an appointment to see Bill Pease to see if we could resolve Gerry Doherty's matter sooner rather than later. In the back of my mind was a nagging worry that the planned NORAID demonstration was going to spin Gerry's problem in an unwanted direction. Bill had worked predominantly in the Civil Division of the Office, dealing mostly with financial issues such as forfeitures, fines, and restitution. I had guessed, accurately, that Bill had "caught" the Gerry Doherty case and was just filling in for a colleague on the Criminal side who was otherwise engaged. And since the Northern District is geographically huge, with many miles of illegal crossing opportunities, illegal entry matters were both plentiful and ordinarily routine. Fortunately, Bill didn't see the case as any big deal, even with the "IRA terrorist bomber" overlay.

Although my practice did not typically bring me into contact with him on a regular basis, Bill and I had had a continuing cordial relationship. Our meeting this day started off on an especially warm note, with me complimenting him on what a good-looking guy he was. This had become a running joke over the prior week (in fact, 35 years later we still laugh over this; it's old to everybody but us) because there was in fact a striking similarity in our appearance at the time. About the same height, we both had a full head of thick curly brown hair and a Tom Selleck-like mustache (which at the time was thought to be quite hip). What made this particularly amusing to both of us was that when we had separately been interviewed by WIXT-9 after Gerry Doherty's first court appearance, the studio editor inserted "Ed Menkin, Defense Attorney" across the bottom of Bill's interview and displayed "AUSA Bill Pease" below mine. (Although it was in fact pretty funny, I did entertain a concern that the NORAID people wouldn't think so and it could feed their latent suspicion of me.)

Despite Gerry's serious prison history (there could be no minimizing it), I tried to have Bill see that the trunk-in-the-car caper was a pretty naïve and clumsy effort and that there really was no danger to the community by Gerry's border crossing attempt. Fortunately for me, Bill was in a fairly benevolent mode, a point of view that was enhanced by his confirmation of Gerry's efforts in both London and Toronto to obtain an entry visa. No terrorist with a criminal record and evil intentions would go to those lengths. We worked out a deal, one that I thought was fair, and something that I thought that Gerry would go for: the Feds would drop the felony charge, let Gerry plead guilty to a misdemeanor, and be sentenced to time served. It was a given that Gerry had to agree to be deported. The bottom line: nice seeing you but you've got to get out of Dodge. I didn't bother to check in with NORAID to see if they were OK with it.

I went to see Gerry at the jail and, as I expected, he accepted the realities and agreed to the proposal. So, 19 days after he was greeted by a border agent with not much of a sense of humor or romance, Gerry pleaded guilty to a misdemeanor (8 U.S. Code § 1325. Improper entry by alien) and Judge Conan sentenced him to time served and sent him on his way. He also had to pay a $25 fine.

The After Party

I thought I had done a pretty good job for Gerry. His visit to America didn't work out exactly as he had planned, but I had helped him avoid a felony conviction and he spent only 19 days in the clink instead of the 5 years he could have gotten. On the whole, Gerry was happy with my efforts and generally satisfied with how things had worked out for him. The folks from NORAID? Well, not so much. They saw the disposition of the case as a premature termination of their chance to protest The Cause and bring further enlightenment to the people of Central New York on the subject of The Troubles.

Despite Gerry's Federal case being technically "over", he was still being held in custody at the Public Safety Building pending his deportation. This coincided nicely with NORAID's demonstration, which they had planned before they learned that Gerry was pleading guilty. On a nice Saturday morning in front of the Public Safety Building, I watched 50 or so protesters march and wave placards crying out "Freedom for Gerry Doherty". And they were pretty angry. I didn't take it in any way as unhappiness over what I had tried to do for Gerry. But it did occur to me that their protest was really not about or even for Gerry Doherty; he was, after all, "free". For them, it was the idea of Gerry Doherty and what he represented. Their guest speaker was a guy who at the time was the Comptroller for Nassau County, an up and coming politico who was closely allied with the Northern Irish cause and, coincidently, was a longtime friend of Maire Dolan. His name was Peter King and later in life he went on to a pretty impressive career, 14 terms in the United States Congress. Peter gave a fiery speech about independence for Northern Ireland and how the British are still running things, even in America:

I thought we had won our freedom from England over 200 years ago! But I have news for you! This country is still taking orders from 10 Downing Street.

It was a great and moving speech. A couple of folks

invited me to speak, but I declined. I didn't think I could add anything to Peter's fiery remarks. And besides, I never could quite figure out what 10 Downing Street had to do with Gerry Doherty.

DANNY'S GENIUS FAKEOUT DEFENSE AND LOUIE THE FROG

Sometimes you gotta do what you gotta do. Pleading a client guilty to a crime is never a fun enterprise but given the reality that The House is almost always holding most of the cards and there aren't any aces left in the deck that are likely to come your way, it's usually the only solution that really works. Most clients are reluctant to face the inevitable; but when you take out a yellow legal pad and fill out two columns, one marked "This Is What You Get If You Plead" and the other marked "This Is What You Could Get If You Don't Plead", certainty starts to look a whole lot more attractive than playing longevity bingo. So most clients accept the inevitable and plead. You do what you gotta do.

But then there are those cases when pleading is out of the question and you've got to go to trial. It's usually for a reason that's not related to the number of months or years at the bottom of the "This Is What You Could Get If You Don't Plead" column; it's more likely to be found in the third column labeled "This Is What Could Happen to You if You Plead and Cooperate." Sometimes it makes more sense to shut up and play Beat the Dealer, on the off chance the Government's case will falter. Sometimes it happens; not often, but sometimes. Even though it didn't work out for us in this particular case, we had to take our shot.

I had this client, Danny M., a slim bearded guy with a sharp mind and a cynical sense of humor. Along with some of his friends, Danny was getting high quality meth from a biker gang in Pennsylvania and retailing it around the Binghamton, New York area. Well, as it usually goes, the DEA busts Danny, and even though he's looking at 5 years in prison, Danny's not enthusiastic about snitching on an armed mob of really dangerous people. So, he tells me he's gonna take his chances and go to trial.

Danny's thinking, not completely illogical, is that if he straight up pleads guilty but doesn't snitch out his biker gang suppliers, he would probably get the maximum sentence of 5 years; if he goes to trial and doesn't snitch out the bikers, and he also gets convicted and he still gets the 5 years, his body remains in operating condition. And besides that, he tells me he thinks he has a great defense. Even though I'm really dubious, I listen to his story.

Danny tells me he worked in a body shop owned by his friend Fran, a quiet and mild-mannered guy with an active imagination. In their inventory, along with sanders, epoxy, and high gloss enamel, they carried small ounces of meth for special customers. Fran and Danny didn't exactly consider themselves to be drug dealers; they paid more serious attention to actually running the body shop which was a convenient money laundering outlet (customers with checks from their insurance company were happy to get a cash discount when they could pocket the overage, so they often paid cash).

The methamphetamine they carried was supplied by Louie

the Frog who got his supply from a biker gang just across the Pennsylvania border. Sometimes Danny accompanied Louie on his PA runs, so he got to know the bikers and they got to know him. Danny and Fran had recently acquired a small-time customer in the person of a guy named Horney when he brought his dented Honda in for repair. Horney knew he could score a little speed from Danny and Fran and after he ran out of dents in his Honda, his visits to the body shop were becoming more frequent. Funny thing: each time Horney showed up it was pretty closely related in time to visits from Louie the Frog making drops to re-up a supply. Danny and Fran missed the coincidence. (The "coincidence" was no surprise to the DEA agents who were employing Horney as an informant.)

One day Horney tells Danny he'd like to move up to some weight, a pound, and he has a crew who can move it for him. Danny and Fran are out of inventory and Louie isn't scheduled to make a biker run to PA for several weeks. Now, even though Louie the Frog spent most of his waking hours eating—and Louie was 400 pounds if he was an ounce—Louie was not without imagination. And for whatever reason, he really doesn't like Danny dealing with Horney and he doesn't mind burning him. So Louie has Danny and Fran go to the store and buy several boxes of Mother Fletcher's Genuine Baking Soda and they spend an afternoon filling up large plastic storage baggies of what could pass for methamphetamine if you looked at it from, say, ten yards away with your sunglasses on and didn't test it or sample it. Danny, who was also tired of Horney coming by, thought this was a genius idea and didn't mind ripping off Horney, a rather wimpy guy who seemed to get a minor thrill out of hanging out with drug dealers.

They agree to a meetup at the HoJo's off route 81. Fran wants to drive. And bring a gun. Danny and Louie the Frog think that the gun idea is a very bad idea but they agree that it'll just be Fran (no gun) and Danny since Horney has never actually met Louie. That night Fran drives Danny over to the HoJo's off route 81 in Louie's extra-large size light blue Lincoln Continental to meet Horney. Danny gets out of the car and goes into HoJo's where Horney is sitting at the counter. Too many people around (it was fish fry night). So Danny tells Horney to meet him at the Burger King parking lot up the road.

They drive over to the Burger King and Fran now decides that since he missed dinner, he's hungry, so they first pull up to the drive-thru and Fran orders a Whopper with extra onions and a large order of fries. Horney is waiting on the other side of the parking lot. Fran pulls over to eat his Whopper and Danny exits the car to walk over to Horney. Horney shows Danny the money and Danny goes back to Fran, who's still eating his Whopper. Danny reaches for a bag that's on the floor but Fran tells him that those are his fries. The baking soda is in a bag in the seat behind him. Danny takes the bag, stuffs it inside his leather jacket and goes back to Horney.

The hand-off goes pretty smoothly except for the part where three DEA agents with guns drawn suddenly appear and remove Danny from Horney's car. Fran never did finish his Whopper; another trio of DEA agents interrupt his meal (for some reason, maybe to entertain their supervisor, the agents duly noted in their DEA-6 reports that when arrested "the subject had both hands on a Burger King Whopper.")

So now Danny is sitting in the back of an unmarked police car and one of the agents pulls out his DEA ID and waves the baggie at him and says to him, "Surprised Danny? You didn't know we were on to you for months, did you?" So Danny says, "Surprise is on you, asshole. That's not drugs." Props to Danny for this moment of transitory bravado. Instead of being terrorized, thinking that this event as perhaps what will turn out to be the lowest point of his life, Danny is thinking he'll be saved by the fact that the "drugs" weren't drugs at all. Ergo, he's not gonna be convicted of a drug sale or possession.

Fran is similarly situated in the back of another police car, and he too is boldly announcing to the agents that "You don't have what you think you have."

Once over their initial limited euphoria, Danny and Fran start to sober up. Their mood isn't brightened much when they learn that the DEA has also rounded up Louie the Frog (I would have paid real money to see how they lassoed him into the back of a police van).

Danny Has Questions but Doesn't Like the Answers

Happily, Danny is granted bail and after a while we meet in my office. After I've got to hear about what a lowdown snake that little Horney guy is and that it's a good thing that he and Louie talked Fran out of bringing a gun, Danny tells me that he's pretty sure we can beat these charges in a walk. Vaguely intrigued and fleetingly considering that maybe I really did waste three years of law school instead of listening to guys like Danny, I inquire into what he thinks the plan ought to be. The drugs weren't drugs! See? The buyer was fake! Get it? Fake buyer? Fake drugs? Danny thinks this is a solid foundation for a winning defense. He thinks we have a genius defense. After what judges reflexively and insincerely call "due deliberation", I tell him I don't think so.

I've already gotten and reviewed the DEA-6 reports. There wasn't just the Burger King buy. There were several surveilled buys with Horney, and he was wearing a wire. Each of the other buys were of real drugs. Not fake. As for the Burger King caper, I try to explain to Danny that under Federal law an attempt to commit a crime is treated the same as committing the crime (it's got to be a real attempt, not just an I'm-thinking-about-it reverie), so whether the drugs were real or not, the back and forth with Horney on the wire was going to satisfy most reasonable people that Danny was attempting to sell meth (fake or not) at the Burger King. Danny tells me this is bullshit and whomever made up a law like this ought to be kicked out of Congress.

Danny's unhappiness with the Rule of Law doesn't end there. I start going over the Indictment with him. There are several counts of conspiracy to possess and distribute methamphetamine (not any great surprise there); there's an additional count of a violation of 18 U.S. Code § 641. Now, just in case you haven't heard of § 641 (I hadn't, and you can be sure Danny hadn't), it's one of these arcane laws that prohibits the theft or embezzlement of public money or property. Public money, public property.

"What are they talkin' about? We didn't steal nothin'."

"Well, it says attempt. They're saying that you attempted to steal Government property."

"What Government property?"

"The money Horney gave you at the Burger King for what

he thought was meth. You don't think it was Horney's, do you? It was the DEA's."

"Well they got it back."

"Doesn't matter. You attempted to steal it."

"Because the drugs weren't drugs and I stole money that I didn't get I'm gonna be charged with a crime? These people are fucking crazy. They just make this shit up as they go along. Who writes these laws?"

The little legal seminar I'm having with Danny does not seem to be moving the needle towards a plea bargain. If anything, it has stiffened Danny's resolve to take the case to trial. The clincher for him is when I tell him that the Feds will agree to a lesser sentence if he cooperates by testifying against Louie the Frog (who was their main target all along). Giving up whatever he knows about the bikers in PA would be bad enough; turning on Louie is out of the question. Danny's not snitching anybody out and we wind up having to go to trial even though I know, and Danny eventually knows, that it's not gonna be much more than a long slow guilty plea.

In Binghamton, the Land of the Slow Guilty Plea

So now we're in a Federal courtroom in Binghamton, New York. The courthouse was one of those granite blockhouses of 1930's architecture, something on the order of an Albert Speer design for von Runstedt just in case he needed a bunker in downtown Binghamton. It started out as a combination Post Office and Courthouse and thereafter a series of offices for federal agencies were Rube Goldberged in, just in case there was additional confusion needed as to the building's purpose or identity. It had an elevator which was outdated about a week after it was installed.

The case was assigned to the Hon. Neal P. McCurn, a tall and courtly man and one of the nicest people I've ever known to wear judicial robes. His pathway to the bench was through his involvement in local politics and large firm insurance litigation. Not a boisterous glad hander, not an overweening former prosecutor with sharp teeth, he was just a very decent guy who genuinely liked people, who respected hard work and good lawyering, and was smart enough to know what he didn't know.

Judge McCurn summoned us to his chambers just before we started the trial. There were five of us: two experienced prosecutors, Greg West and Gary Sharpe (later to become a Federal judge himself), my friends Dave D'Amico, representing Louie, and John DeFrancisco, representing Fran, and me. It probably shouldn't have come as a shock to me—but it did—when Judge McCurn started out with this: "Boys, I know you all have a ton of experience in these kinds of cases, but I want you to know I've never tried a criminal case in my life. So I hope you'll go easy on me." We, of course, were all completely disarmed (which was probably Judge McCurn's intention of course). What were we gonna say? No?

Judge McCurn's candor resonated for me in additional way. Although I had had plenty of criminal trial experience, in truth I had never tried a Federal criminal case to verdict. The procedural differences, I knew, really weren't that great, but there was still a small nagging insecurity that made me a little nervous. Right after our meeting with the Judge, Gary Sharpe, never one to pass up an opportunity to stir up minor mayhem with a practical joke, smilingly informed me that he and Greg were going to split up the Government's opening statement and that I ought to be prepared for that. This, of course, was nonsense and generally not permitted; but he knew that I didn't know that, and he got a major laugh when I started protesting to the Judge. Even McCurn knew that Gary had been pulling my leg and everyone, except me, got a good laugh over it. On that embarrassing note, we commenced the trial of Danny M., Fran the Burger King, and Louie the Frog.

The trial rolled on the way routine drug trials do. We had the usual procession of DEA agents detailing their surveillance of Louie the Frog's activities and Danny and Fran's sales of small amounts of methamphetamine to Horney. We listened to Horney, nervous as a chicken, haltingly recount how he got into trouble, agreed to work as an informant for the DEA, and how he set up buys from Danny and Fran. The guy was a small guy and rather pathetic but we didn't get very far challenging his credibility since everything he said had been captured on a body wire and we were treated to a medley of Danny and Fran's greatest hits when they were played for the jury.

Of course, we had the requisite chemist witness who confirmed that the five buys Horney had made all tested positive for methamphetamine; and the guy was really impressive when he not only identified the Burger King package as containing baking soda but he also identified it as Mother Fletcher's Genuine Baking Soda. (Who knew that cooking ingredients had unique chemical signatures? See, this is the kind of really arcane knowledge one acquires practicing criminal law.)

As predicted, we were going nowhere and Danny was becoming resigned to the inevitable. We suffered a brief episode of bad karma when Danny and Louie--just Danny and Louie—got stuck in the elevator because of "weight overload" and the trial was delayed for two hours because they needed to call in a maintenance crew with special tools. Once we got the trial started again, Danny seemed pleased that I was able to take some shots where I could, but I still thought Danny's Genius Defense was really a nonstarter (when I brought the subject up in my opening the statement, trying to lighten things up, I was met with stone-faced indifference from the jury who seemed to be fixated from the get-go on the three drug dealers sitting before them).

Louie the Frog Rises

Maybe we were wearing our desperation glasses, but still, we were seeing the occasional faint glimmer of hope. The agent who arrested Danny was on assignment in Indonesia and he was the main witness to Louie the Frog's PA runs. So the Government had to make do with his partner, the guy who would write up the reports of the surveillance of Louie the Frog. Part of the problem, albeit a minor one, was that Fran occasionally drove Louie's large light blue Lincoln Continental and although Fran was a good size guy, he didn't remotely resemble Louie the Frog. It's hard to mistake a 400-pound man for anyone other than a 400-pound man. In one of this agent's reports, he characterized the driver of the Lincoln as "a heavy-set white male", strongly implying in the report that it was Louie. We all knew, and by trial time the agent knew, the driver in this incident wasn't Louie at all but rather it was Fran. And I'm trying to cross examine the guy about the general accuracy of his reports compared to what he actually did or saw. I'm doing my best to exploit a minor mistake.

And I'm getting somewhere. He admits it was foggy. He admits he had never seen Fran before. I'm calling into question his powers of observation (because at that point everyone knows it was Fran). So I pulled out his report and I ask him if he wrote that "The subject Miller was a passenger in a light blue Lincoln Continental driven by a heavy-set white male believed to be Louis Fargnoli."

He says yes, he wrote that.

I turn to Louie the Frog who was seated next to us and say, "Louie, stand up willya?"

Louie lumbers laboriously up from his chair.

I say to the witness, "Officer, would you say that this man is heavy set?"

He waits a beat and then says, "Sir, I would say that man is huge."

Well, it was a pretty witty remark and it brought the house down. Even Louie laughed. But, in candor, it didn't amount to much more than momentary entertainment for the jury and after four days of otherwise somber testimony the jury convicted Danny, Fran and Louie the Frog, even on the count of attempting to steal the buy money from the fake buyer buying fake drugs.

Not Quite the End of Things

None of this was much of a surprise.

But there was a surprise in store for us all, a major one. Whether it was the result of Judge McCurn deciding to flex his new-found authority in criminal cases or his simply being unimpressed with the nature and quality of the Government's case against Fran, he tossed Fran's conviction and vacated the jury's verdict. We all liked Fran and we were happy for him.

The Burger King story was sort of endearing and made him out to be, on the surface of things, a good-natured mope who was just along for the ride. In reality, we knew (as Judge McCurn and the prosecutors didn't) that it was Fran's idea to bring a gun to the meeting with Horney (mercifully that didn't come to fruition). We also knew (as Judge McCurn and the prosecutors didn't) that Fran was far deeper into the enterprise than the proof showed. But judicial lightning struck in his favor (a Federal Judge setting aside a guilty verdict is very rare and a very big deal). So we were happy for him. For a while.

Federal Prosecutors are not widely known for their benevolence or their senses of humor (some mutant strains have periodically arisen but they usually don't last long in their jobs). AUSAs Gary Sharpe and Greg West were more than a little unhappy over Judge McCurn's tossing out Fran's conviction. For one thing, it was an unwelcome reminder of who is really in charge in Federal Court (prosecutors get so used to running the show that they get more than a few judges believing it too). They were also unhappy over their need to explain this turn of events to the dozen or so agents who worked the case for a year. And they also secretly believed that Fran was the most vulnerable of the three defendants and the candidate most likely to flip on the biker gang once he was promised leniency when he was facing sentencing. Now all of that was on hold. This was but a temporary disappointment for them.

As I mentioned at the beginning of this saga, the Government is The House and they are rarely out of aces. One particularly nasty little ice axe they have in their backpack when things don't go their predetermined way is the right to appeal in some limited circumstances; and a judge kicking a guilty verdict is one of them. So, true to their calling, the Government appealed Judge McCurn's decision to vacate Fran's conviction, a move that shocked no one but the Burger King himself. And as fate would have it, the Second Circuit Court of Appeals promptly reversed Judge McCurn, reinstated Fran's guilty verdict, and sent him off to prison along with Danny and Louie the Frog.

A few months later, I was walking down the street when I ran into Gary Sharpe. Gary wasn't without a sense of humor although he was a guy more inclined towards the practical joke than subtle irony; I was still stinging from his attempt to persuade me that both he and Greg could both give opening statements in Danny's trial. I teasingly asked him why did he have to go and appeal Judge McCurn's letting Fran go free; I somewhat disingenuously told him that Fran was really a fun guy and that the Government could have let it all go and been satisfied with just hooking Danny and Louie the Frog.

Gary looked at me for a brief moment.

"Hey Eddie, sometimes you gotta do what you gotta do."

I really couldn't argue with the logic.

OPERATION WEED AND SEED GOES OFF THE RAILS

It's the Spring of 1996. I'm sitting at my desk trying to mind my own business and the phone rings. Which, of course, is a good thing; if the phone doesn't ring the chances of getting The Next Big Case go way down. (Today, when my phone rings it's almost always a telemarketer promising to move me up to the Number One slot on Google Search).

The call is from the Federal Court Clerk's Office asking me to take on an assignment of a drug case and asking if I could please show up for a two o'clock arraignment. I'm generally leery of drug cases (for reasons I'll explain later), so I ask what the case is about. The Clerk doesn't have a whole lot of information but tells me that there was a big sweep that morning and 13 defendants were arrested in something called "Operation Weed and Seed". This registers not with me (she doesn't know what it is either), and I ask her what drugs are involved. She tells me it's a crack case. I ask how much crack. She says 0.87 grams. This definitely registers with me. 0.87 grams of crack cocaine is a quantity which could comfortably fit on your fingernail. I ask if she's sure, she says yes.

This is a Federal Indictment over less than a gram of

cocaine? Sure. No problemo. I'll be right over. I have nothing better to do than to take on a minor (and I'm talking minor here) drug case prosecuted by the U.S. Attorney where the standard drill is to show up at arraignment, find out what sentence the Federal Sentencing Guidelines call for, go through the standard motions, only to eventually roll over and plead the guy because in better than 95% of their cases the proof is overwhelming. I dream of cases like this.

The Grand Opening

So I wind up in the Magistrate's courtroom for arraignment on time and find out that this is the debut appearance of something called "Operation Weed and Seed: Syracuse". Since it's a premiere, the U.S. Attorney himself, Tom Maroney, is present. Out from the courtroom's side door comes a multiracial parade of 13 small time (very small time) unhealthy looking miscreants, who are all charged with the sale of miniscule amounts of crack cocaine or conspiracy to engage in such a transaction. The quantities are grams. Not ounces. Not kilos. Grams. The defendants are all bedecked in the same jail-orange jumpsuits and have both handcuffs and leg chains on. They look like they are anxiously awaiting a casting call audition for "Cool Hand Luke" but Paul Newman is nowhere to be found. They are accompanied by a large squadron of U.S. Marshals, sheriffs, and DEA agents, all of whom seem to be playing the role of vaqueros who need to be sure no stray wanders off from the pack.

Before we begin, Tom Maroney takes the floor and in a commanding voice with just the right intonation of basso profundity announces to the Court that these defendants are the first wave of the Weed and Seed Syracuse initiative and that there will be no plea bargaining. They all must plead guilty or go to trial and face long sentences. Tom was my constitutional law professor in law school, a smart and funny guy with a wonderfully deep and resonating voice, one which he never fell out of love with hearing. The guy could talk.

Although there was really no point to his speech (unless it was meant as a press release for the several reporters present) because the arraigning Federal Magistrate Judge couldn't care less, it did serve to ratchet up the attention of the Weed and Seed 13 and their eyes slightly widened with the news that the locomotive of the U.S. Government was intending to bowl right over them, showing no mercy, and demand that they serve long sentences for gram sales of crack cocaine.

Once we are done with the speechifying, the defendants are individually arraigned and, interestingly, there is not one indictment but there are thirteen individual ones. I guess the intention was to reflect the scope of the problem and the range of the investigation by handing down an impressive bunch of indictments. On the other hand, it doesn't require a command of higher mathematics to multiply 13 times 0.87 grams (in truth some of the cases involved as much as 5 grams) and conclude that we have gathered 13 junkies in one mahogany-paneled place and assigned them lawyers at public expense to prosecute cases which cumulatively add up to less than an ounce of crack cocaine. All of them. Cumulatively.

Since this was before a Federal Defender's Office was created, each defendant is assigned a separate attorney. It was probably just happenstance that my case was called last since they seemed to be going in random order, but I got to learn which of my colleagues on the assigned counsel list (in Federal Court it is known as the CJA Panel) was assigned to which of the codefendants. If the defendants seemed to be a disparate group their assigned attorneys matched them in variety. They ranged from the dependably competent and reliable to a clutch of the clueless who should no more be practicing law in Federal court than they should be trusted to successfully complete a 5-item shopping list at the grocery store.

There was once a much beloved Deputy State Supreme Court Clerk named Mahlon Jeffries, a very witty man and a great mimic, who maintained in the pull-out drawer to his desk a well-annotated yellow legal pad emblazoned across the top with the title, "The Worst Lawyers in Onondaga County." After retiring from a 30-year career in the Merchant Marine, Mr. Jeffries brought an informed and world-weary perspective to the day to day parade of truly incompetent lawyers coming in and out of his court, and it didn't take long for him to compile this list. Mr. Jeffries' list was constantly updated and closely held, but he was willing to share it with some judges and some lawyers (at least those lawyers who never made the list). He was not above consulting The List when the judge would knowingly ask for an attorney to be assigned to an especially troublesome and dissatisfied defendant from "Mr. Jeffries' Special List".

Mr. Jeffries was not vindictive and he was nobody's fool. He knew incompetence when he saw it. Perhaps not so curiously, his List generally dovetailed neatly with the less formal catalogue maintained by the defendants incarcerated at the Justice Center. The inmates generally knew who was who on the assigned counsel list and were quick to protest when weeks went by without a jail visit from their assigned attorney or when months went by without seeing any discovery or police or lab reports. Justifiably, what was particularly aggravating to them was when their phone calls were not picked up or answered.

After everyone is arraigned, given the cast and crew (apart from one or two of my colleagues who I highly respected), I don't entertain much of a hope that getting together to discuss matters of mutual interest (like discovery, motions, etc.) is likely to be fruitful.

Michael P. and Aunt Dot

And then I meet my client, Michael P.

Mike was 36, a polite and pleasant guy, but a life-long sad-ass junkie with bad teeth. He had a prior felony conviction (drugs) and a long history of misdemeanor offenses (drugs, drugs, drugs, loitering for drugs, and drugs). He was currently on probation out of County Court for yet another drug conviction. As coincidence would have it, I knew his Aunt Dot, the lady who raised him, and she took time off from her job as a cleaning lady for families in the affluent suburbs to be in court and show her support for her nephew. The arraignment moves pretty quickly, Michael is denied bail (as expected), a motion schedule is ordered, and an early trial date is set (at the request of the prosecution). Michael joins the orange jumpsuit parade trundling out of the courtroom.

Still in the courtroom, I sit down with Aunt Dot. She is a very warm woman and she is worried sick over Michael. She has spent many years being worried sick over Michael. She grieves over his drug addiction. Her concern was especially heightened since this is his first Federal crime and Tom Maroney's early-on speech got her attention big time. She has raised Michael since he was 14 when his mother, Dot's sister, passed away. His father was never really in the picture and is in the wind. I tell Dot what I know about the charges (which isn't much other than it's conspiracy to sell crack cocaine) and feel constrained to tell her that the Feds rarely indict weak cases. I pledge to do my best for Michael and she is grateful.

My first order of business is to find out what the hell Operation Weed and Seed is.

Weed & Seed: Urban Renewal in the Wrong Hands

When Robin Williams once said, "Cocaine is God's way of telling you you're making too much money," he was basically talking to affluent America, white powder, white people. For the urban poor and people of color, the drug of choice back then was crack, a cheaper form of cocaine that was enormously more powerful and far more addictive. Today America is ravaged by addictions to opioids and methamphetamine, but we tend to forget the destructive grip that crack cocaine held on our country back in the 1980's and 1990's. It was an urban crisis that the Government resolved to forcefully address, so it resorted to an historically reliable solution, a real golden oldie which was always believed to work for urban problems: put more people of color in jail.

During the Clinton Administration, a group of Department of Justice officials got it into their heads that passing laws targeting "Superpredators" wasn't sufficient to address violent crime and that there ought to be some kind of ancillary program to really get granular about neighborhood crimes committed by lesser level criminals. Thus was born "Operation Weed and Seed". I'm sure that if you searched the DOJ's archives you'd find at least one memo from the

'90's that escaped the shredder that laid out this genius plan. If a joke started with "A politician, a social worker, and a cop walked into a bar...", I guarantee you that the punchline would be "Operation Weed and Seed."

Let me describe this to you. The plan was to target once-stable inner city neighborhoods which were struggling to maintain a decent level of habitability but had been overtaken by junkies, prostitutes, and the assorted other sad people who prey upon each other (petty drug dealing, street assaults, loitering, relatively minor anti-social conduct) almost all of whom were either addicted to crack or sold it. These undesirable elements would be periodically Blitzkrieged with wholesale sweeping arrests, thus "weeding" the area of these social undesirables. To soften the blow of what might appear to be Government oppression of the poor and people of color, the police effort would then be supplemented by progressive government grants and investments in neighborhood improvements (this would be the "seeding" part of the operation), and this would include housing rehab, landscaping, and the creation of neighborhood involvement through mini-community boards.

A lot of Federal prosecutors lacked the requisite enthusiasm for what they thought should have been street maintenance carried on by the local police, but a DOJ policy was a DOJ policy. Although most Federal prosecutors would deny it, all U.S. Attorney Offices across this our great nation are frequently driven by a political agenda. The U.S. Attorney himself or herself serves by Presidential appointment. To get the gig in the first place, the candidate's got to garner a Palmolive smile from at least one of their United States Senators. And the U.S. Attorney in each District has to answer to the Department of Justice and the Attorney General (who, of course, is also a political appointee of the President). So it's not a great career move for a U.S. Attorney to resist a directive from on high.

Let's say that the Attorney General gets it in his head that Islamic terrorism will be the highest DOJ priority for every one of the 94 U.S. Attorney Offices across the country and he directs all U.S. Attorneys to investigate and prosecute any and all Islamic terrorists and terrorist sympathizers within their respective Districts. Not a terrible or wrong-headed thought; maybe it will make our country safer. But what if you are the U.S. Attorney in Billings, Montana and the only Muslim within a thousand miles—the only one—is the guy who runs the 7-11 on the off ramp of I-90 outside of Missoula? That shopkeeper's not going to have a great couple of weeks.

Like all Utopian visions dancing around in the head of a government bureaucrat, "Operation Weed and Seed" needed a pilot program and Syracuse, New York was chosen as one of a handful of lucky small cities to test the efficacy of the initiative. The U.S. Attorney's Office in the Northern District of New York was very good at prosecuting racketeering, major frauds, complex drug conspiracies, and gun cases; they weren't so hot at urban renewal projects.

For one thing, the "weeding" of small-time neighborhood criminals was heavily dependent on street rips. I'll save you the trouble of looking this up in your copy of the Urban Dictionary. A "street rip" is when an undercover cop makes a surveilled one-on-one buy from a hustler standing on the corner or other trafficked location. The buy made, the deal done, the $10 in cash and the drugs secured in evidence, and the dealer is now in cuffs. Effective, but not likely to scoop up El Chapo or Pablo Escobar no matter how many times you do it. Understandably, the FBI and DEA agents who were used to investigations of greater scope and profundity didn't really want to get with the program, so these rips were detailed to local "task forces", amalgamations of local sheriffs, police detectives, and state troopers who didn't mind the O.T. and got off on the fact they had a federal badge to go along with their snappy looking "Federal Task Force" windbreakers.

The Case Against Michael P.

By the next morning, the Federales have supplied me with a sheaf of police reports, one of which details Michael's involvement in the "conspiracy".

The case against Michael P. is pretty simple: Two Task Force undercover detectives, masquerading as citizens looking to get high, pull into the parking lot of a low-rise apartment complex on the far east end of James Street. This part of James Street, which, back in the day, had rows of handsome houses occupied by the affluent, had been victimized by the kind of urban blight which Weed and Seed was designed to target and eradicate and it is now infested with pockets of junkies, dealers, prostitutes, and the socially undesirable poor (today they are called homeless people).

Standing there is Michael P., jonesing in a bad way, and the coppers can see that this is a junkie badly in need of a fix. Police logic being what it is, they assume that if Mike is jonesing he must know where the drugs are to be found (truly, in this apartment complex you could knock on almost anyone's door and come across somebody's stash) and they ask him where to get some rock (crack cocaine). Michael points to a second-floor balcony and says, "Freddie in 2B" and then volunteers to take them to Freddie B's apartment. The undercovers go up to 2B. Mike knocks on the door, introduces them to Freddie B. and leaves. The cops consummate an $80 buy from Freddie and are back in the parking lot in less than 10 minutes. Michael sees them coming, walks over to their car and asks for "a taste" (one of the vials they've copped from Freddie). This is Michael P.'s undoing if any undoing was even required at that point.

Asking for "a taste" is, to the cops, Michael P's confirmation that he is a "steerer" for Freddie. Michael P. is, therefore, an accomplice and a coconspirator in Freddie's crack business. In the following weeks, the cops make two more buys from Freddie in 2B but they don't see Michael again until they descend on the James Street apartment complex some weeks later to scoop up Freddie, Mike, and the 11 other junkie-dealers they had made small buys from. This minor key dragnet then becomes breathless front-page news for Tom Maroney and his Office when they proudly announced the launch of Operation Weed and Seed. Urban renewal and peace on earth (or at least a section of James Street) are sure to follow.

I go to the jail and meet with Mike. Understandably, he doesn't really remember any of it but doesn't deny any of it either, "Shit, man, all I wanted was a taste. Everybody know Freddie." He definitely denies he was in business with Freddie and he is sure that the only crack cocaine he ever got from Freddie he had to pay for. When I tell him that the Feds want a plea and three years out of his life (his prior record is an escalator for them), all he says is "Man, that ain't right."

I've got to agree with him.

Last Man Standing

About a month goes by and the twelve other defendants have now pleaded guilty. Even the ones who had good lawyers. Each of them probably had their reasons but the swiftness with which they did it bothered me. On the other hand, it was none of my business and I intended to take my time, especially because the proposed three year bid wasn't sitting right with Michael or me given what was really his peripheral involvement in a "conspiracy" to sell less than a gram of cocaine.

His crime is clearly driven by one thing and one thing only: he's an addict. I try my hand at sentence bargaining with Charlie Roberts, the Assistant U.S. Attorney assigned to the case, suggesting a treatment diversion, but all he does is kick it upstairs to Maroney's Chief Assistant Joe Pavone, someone who fancied himself as "an old-time street lawyer" (I think Joe once represented a guy who was being court-martialed when Joe was a JAG officer in the military, but contemporaneous research never did uncover any other citizen Joe had previously defended). Joe was ordinarily good company until you had to ask for a lenient disposition. In those instances, he was known to me and a host of other lawyers as "Dr. No." In any case, I recognized that Tom Maroney's sweeping pronouncement at the beginning of the case was being taken as everyone's marching order for the Weed and Seed cases and it was, indeed, plea or try, max sentence. No bargaining.

The case is assigned to Judge Howard G. Munson, a judge who was not just widely respected but idolized by the defense bar. Funny, smart, intolerant of fools and careless lawyers (especially prosecutors), Munson had tried hundreds of cases before he became a Federal District Court Judge. He was that rarest of members of that fraternity, someone who had never been a prosecutor and therefore never got used to asking or demanding that a defendant go to jail. My thinking was that if Michael P. went to trial and got convicted, Munson could/would decide his sentence himself, without the U.S. Attorney having his thumb on the scale with a negotiated plea bargain. I trusted Munson's wisdom and compassion.

Apart from Judge Munson's hoped-for beneficence in sentencing if Michael P. was convicted, there was another, better reason to opt for trial. I did a little poking around and found out that the twelve other mopes who had promptly pleaded guilty in the Weed and Seed juggernaut were all actual sellers. Small time sellers, but sellers nonetheless. Mike's case was the only one brought against a steerer-accomplice and, when you thought about it, there was at least an argument that Mike had no connection with Freddie B. other than knowing he was selling crack out of his apartment. The facts, of course, were the facts, but I thought there was at least a reasonable way of looking at them for a jury to conclude that Mike's interactions with the undercovers were nothing more than a way to get high, something which sadly defined his life.

The ABC's of a Drug Sale Case

Not to put too fine a point on it, but proving a street rip case is ordinarily child's play for any prosecutor. It's beyond simple. You could do it blindfolded if you had to and you'd only need two witnesses. Witness #1 is the undercover cop who made the deal with the defendant to purchase the item

(Exhibit A). There might be someone else, maybe his cop colleague who witnessed the transaction, or something else, say a tape (audio or video) to prove what Witness #1 has just said. But juries tend to believe police witnesses and you could proceed ahead with just your cop alone if you had to. Witness #1 then identifies Exhibit A which he got from the defendant and shows the jury the form he filled out which proves that Exhibit A was locked in an evidence vault and submitted to the police lab.

Then Witness#2 comes along, the chemist in the police lab who took Exhibit A out of the evidence locker vault and tested it. Witness #2 also signs the form that Cop Witness#1 originally submitted and that paperwork (let's call it Exhibit B) is now the chain of custody form which follows the evidence. It notes the time and date that someone has custody of Exhibit A and it could turn out to be a fairly detailed in-and-out list of activities (out of the lab and into the Grand Jury; back to the lab; out to court; back from court). The idea is that Exhibit A has been carefully shepherded by trustworthy and knowledgeable individuals since it left the grimy hands of the drug-dealing lowlife defendant. And, of course, whilst Exhibit A was in the custody of Witness#2, the lab chemist, it was subjected to all manner of tests (some more sophisticated than others) to prove that Exhibit A is what the prosecutor claims it is: drugs. So, Cop Witness#1 says I bought these drugs (Exhibit A) from the defendant and Lab Witness#2 comes in and says, yep, dem's drugs.

There can be numerous variations of this scenario, depending on the players, the circumstances, and the drugs, but it's the same story. Over, and over, and over. That's one of the reasons I tried to avoid drug cases as my career evolved. I didn't have any principled moral aversion to the conduct of possessing or dealing drugs (well, I did recognize and accept it was illegal and socially unacceptable); it's just that the trials tended to be boring repetitions of the same story on autopilot. The only interesting or challenging parts tended to be Fourth Amendment issues (wiretaps, search warrants, stop and frisk issues) but once you got past that it was pretty much the same old same old until you swiftly arrived at sentencing (which itself is not a lot of fun). And as the years went on the Government got better and better at putting together search warrant and wiretap applications, so those parts of the cases, which were once challenging and interesting, became not much more than a tired slog uphill with no reward.

Trial Prep

As the trial drew near, my preparation efforts intensified. In many ways, trial work is performance art but even a fifteen-minute opening statement takes hours of preparation. When you actually have a point to make on cross-examination (for some lawyers this never happens), preparing for even a short incisive set of questions can take days. So it was with Michael P.'s case. Obviously, the guy had a lot at stake. Three years in the slam for selling less than a gram of crack cocaine is serious business and whether I was assigned or retained, I was going to give him my best effort

Lawyers have a tendency to pick up really arcane knowledge in preparing for a case. It's stuff that neither they nor anyone else will care about after the case is over and it's trivia that would clear the backyard at your neighbor's barbeque if you brought it up in idle conversation. But mercifully, once the case is completed, an invisible flush handle alongside your brain is activated and the trivial knowledge fades then disappears from your consciousness. So it was that in preparing for Michael P.'s trial I came to know that there's cocaine and then there's crack cocaine.

I had never really given much thought to the difference. Had no need to. But the Weed and Seed cases were about crack cocaine specifically. This was 1996 and the draconian injustice of the Reagan Administration's distinction between powder cocaine (you know, the blow that high-end Hollywood agents put up their nose) and crack cocaine (the potent and cheaper rock form which was far more accessible to people of color in the urban pockets of poverty across America) is what drove sentencing in Federal courts. Back then, possession of crack cocaine was treated one hundred times more harshly than possession of an equal amount of powder cocaine. That this disparity had a grossly disproportionate impact on people of color bothered Congress not one little bit (the 100:1 disparity in sentencing was finally remedied by the Fair Sentencing Act of 2010 – after being enforced since 1986).

But it was a strange and curious fact that although under Federal law the penalties for possession or distribution of crack cocaine were enormous and breathtakingly magnified over the penalties for possession or distribution of powder cocaine, under New York State law no distinction was made and the penalties were the same. You could view this difference as an "enlightened" view of the drug problem by one jurisdiction over the other but, clearly, if you had to be prosecuted over a crack cocaine offense, you'd much prefer that the case stay local and not go Federal. Obviously, Mike P. had no choice in which court he was being prosecuted, so the fact that he was facing draconian justice in Federal Court was just his bad luck.

But another, and far more determinative, part of the luck of the draw here was that the Feds relied on the Syracuse Police Lab for their drug testing. Given the big picture, the Feds were not going to spend their lab resources (the FBI lab, the DEA lab) on what was otherwise a pipsqueak set of drug cases. This made a major difference because, as I said earlier, New York State treated powder cocaine the same as crack and, at least on one level, the SPD lab ordinarily didn't test for crack; they could, but to them, cocaine was cocaine.

Therefore, most of my attention in trial prep was drawn to the lab reports. There were 13 separate cases, some involving multiple street rips, but the drugs were all submitted to the same place for testing: the Syracuse Police Lab. Their chemist, Karen Stagnitta, had done the testing on all 13 cases and she had generated a sheaf of reports, all of which had been supplied to me. (Even though 12 of those cases had nothing to do with Michael P or Freddie in 2B, I asked for them to get a sense of the big picture). They all said the same thing: the substances tested in each case were "cocaine base" (crack cocaine).

Along with the reports themselves (which are basically fill-in the blank forms with a signature attesting to and certifying the accuracy of the findings) was another sheaf of Stagnitta's notes. These consisted of graphs and some copied pages from the Lab Log Book. In all, this paperwork came to about 50 pages. I read all of it, hoping there'd be something to work with. After some hours of bleary-eyed reading, I found something that I instinctively knew would be a game changer. Jackpot.

In order to put a point on the dagger, I needed some additional documents and the assistance of the Court. So I went to see Judge Munson in his chambers, without the U.S. Attorney present, and I explained to him what I had found. He got it right away and acted somewhat bemused. I asked him to order the production of the one-page notation in the Court's record which showed the date and time the Grand Jury reported out the Indictment against Michael P. (this document, while not secret, is something you don't ordinarily have access to). I also asked him to order the production of the lab reports which were presented to the Grand Jury as exhibits (I wanted the originals, not copies). I also wanted a Subpoena Duces Tecum for the FBI Agent who brought the certified SPD Lab reports over to the Grand Jury and swore that he got them on a particular day. And, for good measure, I asked him to order the production of the original SPD Lab Log Book, a bound diary-like tome which has, listed by sequential date upon each page, the testing which was done on each submitted case. (I had copies of some excerpted pages but wanted the whole thing even though the Log Book wasn't supposed to leave the Lab.) Judge Munson granted all of my requests. The trial was a week away.

The Trial of Michael P.

The trial started. I was expecting the traditional street rip template story and the prosecutor, Assistant United States Attorney Charlie Roberts, didn't disappoint. Of course, since this wasn't strictly speaking a street rip case (the street rip was with Freddie B and Mike was supposed to be his steerer), the focus of the police testimony is their interactions with Mike in the parking lot both before and after the undercovers buy their crack from Freddie B. We probably spend too much time with Charlie getting the cops to explain their Operation Weed and Seed mission (I objected as irrelevant and prejudicial; Charlie argued it was necessary "context and background". Judge Munson let him go with it for a little while.)

The testimony got down to the actual conversations and conduct in the parking lot and both cops agreed that Mike was junkie-high agitated, did not offer to sell them drugs, was not known then to have had drugs (except, of course in his bloodstream), and did not otherwise show up on their radar during their month-long investigation. And they couldn't place or connect him with either Freddie B. or Freddie B.'s apartment other than knowing where it was and then introducing them to Freddie. He was, I was trying to show the jury, just a sad-assed junkie with no skin in the game other than his plea that these two guys share a "taste" of their recent crack acquisition from Freddie B.

On the whole I was pretty satisfied with how it went with the cop witnesses. By the end of Day 1, I felt we were still alive.

We knocked off at about 4:00 P.M., plenty of time for Judge Munson to start his series of Manhattans for the evening at Sterio's Landmark, his favored watering hole down the street. (These would supplement his lunchtime Manhattans; but, truth to tell, for as long as I knew him—and I knew him long and well—he may have been a legendary drinker but I never once knew of his drinking to get in the way of doing his job.) He invited me to come along, but there were no Manhattans at Sterio's for Eddie that day.

I still had the lab evidence and lab chemist to prepare for. After all, even though the cops didn't get the crack cocaine from Michael, they still had to show that Freddie's product was not just "cocaine" but crack cocaine. Inconveniently for me, the discovery provided by the Government showed that all of the drugs that the Operation Weed and Seed Task Force had gathered up was crack cocaine; all of the 13 different lab reports for all 13 of the defendants' cases showed it. It was the main reason even my more experienced colleagues had pled their clients promptly. Cop Witness #1 makes buy; Lab Person Witness #2 says it's crack. Name of tune, end of story.

But something about the lab reports had caught my attention as I had prepared for trial. It was the date on the lab report and the date on the Indictment.

Good News and Bad News: Your Lab Results Are Back

As expected, Charlie called the SPD Lab Chemist, Karen Stagnitta, a young woman with a pleasant and earnest manner and a thousand-watt smile. Charlie's direct examination was quite standard, right out of the prosecution play book for drug cases. Who are you? What's your job? How much education and training have you had? Has your testimony been previously accepted as that of an expert? Did you perform the required testing on the suspected controlled substances the police submitted to you in this case? What precautions and procedures did you take to secure the integrity of the evidence? What tests did you perform? Can you explain each of those tests to the jury? Did you reach a conclusion as to the identity and nature of this evidence? Do you have an opinion based upon a reasonable degree of scientific certainty as to the identity and nature of this evidence? So, it's cocaine base, is that right? Crack cocaine? Thank you very much.

I don't think I objected or interrupted one time. I just let the two of them blithely roll with the script and the program. Perhaps a bit smug in my confidence, I'm sitting there thinking—knowing--that I'm the Santa Fe Chief hurtling down the tracks at 115 mph directly at them and neither Charlie nor Stagnitta have a clue about what's coming.

So, I start in on my cross-examination and at first seem to be engaged in the tired and all too common "stratagem" of simply repeating what the witness has already told the jury on her direct testimony. It's truly astounding to me how many lawyers do this; it's pointless and almost always destructive because all you seem to be doing is reinforcing what your adversary has already established. But I knew exactly what I was doing, and my intention was to irretrievably lock Stagnitta into her version of laboratory reality.

We start in with how you initially identify cocaine in the lab. It's called the Scott Reagent test and it's so basic and simple that any officer can do in his squad car after making a buy or seizing suspected drugs. You just add a magic elixir of chemicals to a sample in a test tube and if the colors of pink and blue show up, the news is not that it is boy and girl twins but rather that the substance is cocaine. It's pretty crude and it's only a presumptive test; it's not conclusive but it is widely accepted and used. Stagnitta is happy to tell the jury about it and how it's done and I'm happy for the information. She tells us how much time it took to do the Scott Reagent test on all of the 13 Weed and Seed cases which were submitted.

Next, I give her the chance to explain the advanced testing she engaged in on this case and although it's pretty standard stuff, known to all criminal lawyers, prosecutors, and cops, it all sounds mighty science-voodoo to the jury. This is when you submit a sample to a method of testing called gas chromatography/mass spectrometry. And Stagnitta explains this interesting alchemy to the jury:

A small amount of sample is dissolved in a solvent. This could be chloroform or methanol. It is injected into an instrument called a gas chromatograph, or GC, for short. In the GC there is a column which is circular and you have a solution vaporized in the gas state, it goes around the column, that is where you have the components of the substance separated. So that is where the separation occurs.

Then it goes to another instrument, which is called a mass spectrometer and the simplest way to look at that is you have electrons bombarding this molecule of something and as a result the molecule breaks up into various fragments so you have these fragments which produce ions so you are looking at characteristic ions for that particular substance and each substance has characteristic ions.

You then go to your handy ion reference chart and find out what chemical signature you are looking at, because all drugs have different ionic signatures. And in this case, voila! ladies and gents of the jury, the ionic signature comes back as exactly what we suspected: it's cocaine! She then tells us how much time it took to do the gas chromatography/mass spectrometry tests on all of the 13 Weed and Seed cases which were submitted.

But, wait! There's more! As we have already learned, there's cocaine and then there's cocaine base. What we know as "cocaine" is actually "cocaine hydrochloride"; for it to become cocaine base—crack—the hydrochloride molecule has to be removed. (The simple learning is that all cocaine base is cocaine, but not all cocaine is cocaine base. That's why it's called "base".)

So, at the risk of putting the jury into a further deep sleep, I get Stagnitta to tell us that there is but one--and only one—way to tell if a suspected drug is cocaine base and not just cocaine and that is to put it through further testing called infrared spectroscopy, a sophisticated method that employed something that looked like a toy oven for Barbie's playhouse but which measured wavelengths of light emitted by organic compounds:

> Organic compounds absorb IR infrared light at specific wavelengths due to their structure that allows you to identify the organic compound based on its absorption pattern that you get. With cocaine, you can have cocaine base or you can have cocaine hydrochloride. These two compounds have slightly different structures; therefore, they have different infrared or IR spectra.

So, after this Bill Nye the Science Guy seminar and hoping against hope that I haven't lost the jury here (Munson is following all of it because he knows where I'm going; Charlie has remained clueless up until this point and thinks I'm just wasting time), I moved on to my jackpot question:

> Q: Didn't you also tell us that no competent professional reliable chemist would ever offer an

opinion that a substance was cocaine base based exclusively on the Scott Reagent Test and gas chromatograph/mass spectrometer test, isn't that right?

A Yes.

I loved this question. It was the point I had been working towards after an hour of cross-examination and the point I had been anticipating after five days of trial preparation. You can't tell if a drug is cocaine base without the IR test. I was so in love with the question—and Stagnitta's answer—I asked it twice.

And then, the payoff: Stagnitta had certified the 0.87 grams as cocaine base on March 26, 1996, and her report, which she swore to, then went to the Grand Jury, which considered that evidence and voted an Indictment which was filed with the Court at 2:15 P.M. on March 27, 1996. But her own notes and the SPD Lab Log Book showed that she performed the IR testing on all 13 samples on all 13 Weed and Seed cases (including Michael P.'s) during the *entire day* of March 27, 1996. This was what I had earlier disclosed to Judge Munson and he instantly understood and appreciated the gravity of the misstep by the Government and its chemist. She had signed a sworn lab report attesting to something as being true at a time when it was impossible to know if it was true or not. The upshot was that a falsified lab report had been submitted to the Grand Jury.

Q. Ms. Stagnitta, it is possible, is it not, that all of these records [the March 26 reports] are, in fact, accurate and that you wrote down and concluded that these drugs were cocaine base before you ran the infrared, isn't that possible?

A That is not possible, no.

Well, dear, it was not only "possible", it was a 24karat, undeniable fact. Whether it was through inadvertence, mistake, or sheer incompetence, Stagnitta had certified the drugs as crack (on March 26) when, by her own admission, "no competent chemist" would have done so without running the IR spectroscopy which was done on March 27. There was no way out of this. It wasn't a simple matter of mistakenly writing down the wrong date; not only had Stagnitta signed and dated the form to be March 26, but the report was countersigned by the lab supervisor as March 26. And the lab report could not have reflected that the IR testing had been completed on March 27 (which is when it happened according to Stagnitta's notes), because the Grand Jury had already by then voted to return an Indictment that day (March 27) and it had considered the false March 26 reports as proof and evidence that it was cocaine base (crack) that came from Freddie B.

Ba-boom

What we were left with was a hot mess. Stagnitta left the stand deeply embarrassed and feeling disgraced. Judge Munson knew that the Grand Jury presentation of the case against Michael P. was deeply flawed and he reserved his decision on my Rule 29 Motion to dismiss the case (Rule 29 Motions are made at the end of the prosecution's case and basically argue that the Government has failed to even create a jury question; they are routinely made and routinely denied.).

I actually felt a little badly for Charlie Roberts; he had been handed the file only the week before the trial and was told it would be a layup. Didn't work out that way. Mike had followed the proceedings, of course, and while the technical aspects of the lab report evidence seemed to be going way over his head, he knew enough to know things were looking good for us.

So I made my Rule 29 Motion and, perhaps not so shockingly, Charlie had literally nothing to say. Judge Munson reserved his decision and we broke for lunch.

We resumed around 1:30 and Charlie walks in in the company of both U.S. Attorney Tom Maroney and his Chief Assistant Joe Pavone. They huddled briefly in the back of the courtroom until Judge Munson took the bench. Charlie gets up and *he* moves for dismissal under Rule 29 and Judge Munson dismisses the case against Michael P. And that, as they say, was that.

Well, not exactly.

The After-Party

Mike P. was, of course, ecstatic over the charge being dismissed. So too was Aunt Dot. The Government? Well, not so much.

Having a very minor drug case dismissed would ordinarily be taken in stride by the U.S. Attorney, even if it was an embarrassingly negative stat on the Operation Weed and Seed scorecard. But the Office had deeper and wider concerns. The news that Stagnitta had crashed and burned in the only Weed and Seed case that went to trial got around the courthouse pretty quickly. As the U.S. Attorney had feared and predicted, those 12 other cases where the Weed and Seed defendants had previously swiftly pleaded guilty all suddenly came rushing back on the Court calendar, each defendant now claiming that he had been prosecuted on the basis of a set of phony lab reports (you may recall that Stagnitta had done the testing for all 13 Weed and Seed cases and all at the same time). The Government had to beat each one of those motions off with a stick; it created a lot of work but eventually they succeeded. The Court ruled that the defendants would have to live with their deals since by pleading guilty each of them waived any challenge he might have had to the integrity of the evidence against him.

But even that was not the Government's biggest problem.

Nearly 50 years ago, the Supreme Court laid down a rule in a case called Giglio v. United States which required that prior to trial the Government had to disclose to the defense any evidence which would reasonably call into question the credibility of a person the Government intended to call as a witness. Stagnitta's missteps in the Michael P. Weed and Seed case fell squarely into that category. So, every time—that's every time—the U.S. Attorney prosecuted a drug case in the future for which Stagnitta had done the lab work, they would have to disclose to the defendant a bucketload of dirty laundry which they had hoped would have been left in a back room somewhere. To avoid this complication, and needless embarrassment, the solution that the U.S. Attorney's Office hit upon was to try to see to it that Stagnitta was kept away from any Federal cases that might wander into the Syracuse Police Laboratory. After all, they did have another chemist to do the work. What then ensued was a high-level meeting to settle the matter that turned into a major turf war with voices raised and noses becoming severely bent out of shape and the Syracuse Police telling the U.S. Attorney that they would run their lab any way they chose to and that the Feds ought to mind their own business. The harshness and stand-off lasted several months until Karen Stagnitta resolved the issue by leaving the employ of the SPD Lab.

Thus endeth the short-lived era of Operation Weed and Seed. At least I think it ended. I never heard about it again. And you can also rest assured that I never again got another call from the Federal Court to "help out" on a Weed and Seed case.

That was nearly 25 years ago. I recently drove past the 1000 block of James Street, home to Mike and Freddie B. It still looks pretty much the same to me.

DEATH DUTY

The first time I saw a dead body wracked by violence I was about ten years old. A neighbor had leaped to her death from the roof of a six-story apartment building and her impact on the pavement resulted in a bloody mess that was hard to look at. And hard not to look at. Especially for 10-year-old eyes. I guess it was a necessary initiation into how the world goes and a reminder that violence can be visited upon us with very little forewarning. The next time I had the occasion to witness something like that it was 25 years later. And this time I had plenty of forewarning.

It was August 1978, and I was only a few months into my job as an Assistant District Attorney. I was excited to be on the verge of doing "real" cases instead of the motions and appeals they had started me out with when I was a mere law clerk. My pal and law school classmate Bill Fitzpatrick, a year ahead of me at the office, had cleared a path for me with the higher ups. On this particular night I was covering for Fitz—just for that one night--on "death duty", a 24-hour responsibility where you carried a pager and got buzzed when a suspicious death or a genuine homicide required the on-scene presence of an ADA. Since Syracuse wasn't exactly the south side of Chicago, catching death duty ordinarily didn't

One Through the Heart

entail much more than preparing yourself to be inconvenienced on some rare occasion.

This particular day was uneventful, and I had returned home late, as usual, for a quiet dinner with my wife Laurie. Our life was happy and uncomplicated; we were awaiting the birth of our first baby, and our evenings were usually spent watching a few hours of television. We were just settling in to watch Johnny Carson's monologue so I'm guessing it was around 11:30. The pager went off and I called the number. I reached a woman from the 911 call center whose voice and demeanor seemed to convey nothing more dramatic than a report of traffic congestion on Henry Clay Boulevard. She told me that there was a reported homicide in Skaneateles, that the New York State Police were on the scene, and that they were requesting a D.A.'s presence. The only other thing she knew was that a 16-year-old kid had shot his mother. I was given an address.

Though her manner was very routine and businesslike, my reaction was somewhat akin to being told to report immediately to my draft board and that I was shipping out to Viet Nam in the next half hour. I had only been in the office for 6 months and had no clue what would be expected of me at the scene of a homicide. I had been a teacher for 10 years before I attended law school, and about the most intense moment I had experienced in that time was a confrontation with a kid I gave a "D" to on his essay exam. Crime scenes and dead bodies were things I had imagined, read about, or seen on T.V. When I took the death duty pager from Fitz that morning I hadn't thought about anything other than helping a colleague out so he could take the night off.

I got into our car, a red Volkswagen. It wasn't much of an

official looking kind of vehicle to arrive at a crime scene in and that thought only added to my growing anxiety. Skaneateles is a tony bedroom community about a 45-minute drive from Syracuse, the kind of quaint mostly upper middle class village that Hallmark Cards would have invented if it hadn't already existed. Crime was nearly unheard of and homicide unthinkable.

It was a very hot night, and as I drove west I noticed a gigantic moonrise behind me that dominated the eastern horizon to where I felt like it was about to roll over me and everything in its path. It was still looming low in the hot night sky when I came upon the address I had been given.

I expected a small armada of flashing red lights and for the property to be festooned in yellow police tape. There was tape across the driveway and trees in front, but otherwise nothing. Just an unnerving quiet and two unoccupied blue and yellow State Police cruisers parked on the shoulder of the road with their lights off.

I stood in the driveway, uncertain of what to do. It was mystifying to me why no one seemed to be around. It's nearly comical to remember that this was a time when cellphones were unheard of, so I thought for the moment I was really stranded. Suddenly, two tall State Troopers in genuine Rough Rider kit came around from the side of the house and silently approached me. The taller of the two, Jamie Matthews, asked "You from the D.A.'s Office?" and before I had a chance to respond said, "They probably want you at the substation. They took the kid there."

Spooky as the whole scene was, and as inexperienced as I might have been, I surprised myself by assuming a more authoritative demeanor than I had thought I was capable of, and asked them, "Can you brief me on what the story is here?"

It was a pretty grim story. Trooper Matthews and his partner, Bob Gilooly, were first responders to the farmhouse and had gotten what information they could from the boy. From what they knew, and it only came in pieces, it appeared that the boy lived with his divorced mother at the farmhouse. She had come home around 9:30 from late grocery shopping to find all the lights in the house were out. When she came through the darkened kitchen entrance, she must have put the grocery bag and her keys on the kitchen table (they were still there) only to realize the boy was sitting at the table, silently staring at her, and pointing a pump action 12 gauge straight at her.

What words were exchanged, if any, were unknown, but the brutal reality of what happened next was undeniable. The boy ordered his mother to go down the hallway and into a large bathroom, and then directed her to step into the claw-footed bathtub. Again, it was unknown what words were exchanged, what terror or tears the mother expressed, if there was any conversation at all, or how long all of this took, but the boy blasted his mother full in the face with a 12 gauge deer slug and then when she lay crumpled in the bathtub, he emptied the gun into her. It was a breathtakingly bloody mess. The boy then went back into the kitchen, put the shotgun on the table, called 911, and sat down. When Matthews and Gilooly showed up, he was seated at the kitchen table, sobbing.

Just as they finished the debrief, Matthews' car radio squawked. It was BCI Investigator Milt White, the senior detective on the case, calling from the State Police Substation.

He had been questioning the boy and wanted to know if Sergeant Dick Sparrow, their chief forensic evidence investigator, and an ultra-serious guy, had shown up at the house yet. Sparrow was going to be delayed since he had responded to a double fatal DWI accident on the other side of the County. White also related that Senior District Attorney Norm Mordue, the chief of the D.A.'s felony trial unit, and certainly my senior and supervisor, was there at the substation and taking charge of the investigation.

This was an enormous relief to me. It meant I did not have to continue to pretend to be a voice of authority or even worry about command investigative decisions such as a search warrant or evidence gathering. Norm was not just my boss, but a hero and mentor to me. A decorated Viet Nam Veteran with a Purple Heart, a Bronze Star, and the Distinguished Service Cross, he had tried every major homicide the Office had had for many years. He was a good, solid guy with a sense of humor (he was a great mimic) and a willingness to take the time to help younger lawyers. Norm got on the call and told me that I should stay at the scene until Sparrow showed up and then come over to the substation. This last piece was classic Norm Mordue. He could have told me he had this caper and I should go home. But even though I would be of little use or assistance for the rest of the evening, he recognized this as an important learning experience for me and he generously invited me inside as an observer.

Motivated now more by curiosity than responsibility, I told Matthews that I wanted to look inside the house. Exchanging a long glance with Gilooly, Matthews hesitated and then said "OK, but don't touch anything. Sparrow will have a shitfit if he finds out anything's been moved."

The house was completely dark and we moved around quietly, guided by Matthews' flashlight. I felt like a burglar stealthing around a place I wasn't supposed to be. The grocery bag and car keys were on the corner of the table nearest the door. The shotgun remained on the other edge of the table. Nothing seemed disturbed or broken or tipped over. The troopers brought me to the bathroom doorway. Matthews asked if I had ever seen a gunshot victim before and when I told him no he said, "Well, this isn't pretty."

They didn't have to tell me not to step into the bathroom, but I could clearly see what I needed to see from the doorway. A handful of red spent shotgun shells lay side by side on the tiled floor. The strong smell of spent gunpowder still lingered. Moonlight filtered through the three small windows above the bathtub, and even without Matthews' flashlight I could see dark splashes on the wall below the shower head and a wide pattern of bold and thick staining where the tiles met the edge of the tub. The woman's wrecked and bloody body was fully clothed, and she lay lengthwise, completely inside the tub. The shower curtain had been pulled all the way back and since nothing seemed to be broken, disturbed, or torn, it wasn't difficult to theorize that she had gotten into the tub herself (given that there was a lot of blood about five feet up the wall, it indicated that she was probably standing when first shot).

When the flashlight illuminated her head and chest, it cast a stark and cruel light onto what was a ghastly sight. Her head was cleaved down the center. What remained of the left side of her face sunk well below the right side, giving her the grim asymmetrical appearance of a Modigliani sculpture which had been doused in a good deal of blood. There didn't appear to be much left of her chest. After the briefest pause, enough to validate for Matthews and Gilooly that I was making an assessment and not just gawking, I told them I had seen enough and we went out to the driveway to await the arrival of Sergeant Dick Sparrow.

We stood in silence for a few minutes, me to compose myself and the troopers becoming impatient for the arrival of Sparrow. I don't know if it was in an effort to relieve the tension or just a way to demonstrate for me that grim as this scene was it was just another day at the office for these guys, but Matthews started telling Gilooly how funny the previous weekend's Saturday Night Live show was and he then broke into a pitch perfect rendition of The Festrunk Brothers, the two wild and crazy guys who were portrayed by Dan Ackroyd and Steve Martin. It would have been funny to me, even hilarious, had I not been concentrating on suppressing the upset which arose from what I'd just seen. Gilooly was cracking up (Matthews was a very entertaining guy, a fact which was confirmed by my several encounters with him later in my career). I just turned away.

Sparrow showed up. He didn't offer any apologies for being late. He had a reputation for being all business and was very good at his job. He had been briefed in detail by White on his way over and knew exactly what he wanted to accomplish, which was to completely photograph the scene and take possession of the shotgun, the shells, and any other physical evidence they could identify. This wasn't exactly a whodunit. All White wanted from Sparrow was evidence which would corroborate the kid's confession to shooting his mother in the dark bathroom.

Forensics in 1978 wasn't anything like the modern-day version of CSI on television, but Sparrow knew what he was doing and immediately broke out his evidence bags and photographic and video equipment (a set of heavy and clunky apparatuses which were carried around in large metal suitcases; the camcorder hadn't been invented yet and the idea of a cell phone video camera had yet to dawn on Steve Jobs who was then probably still working out of his garage). Sparrow seemed to know who I was and also seemed to know I had gone into the house, neither of these facts doing much to either impress him or lighten his disposition. His entire manner radiated "Stay out of my way", and Matthews and Gilooly, who knew the drill, stood aside. They then silently accompanied Sparrow into the house. It was clear that I was neither invited nor welcome, so I just stood in the moonlight at the end of the gravel driveway for a few more minutes, composing myself.

There was no need for me to remain at the farmhouse. Not sure if protocol or courtesy required me to say goodbye to the troopers ("Thank you so much Trooper Matthews for a lovely evening and tour of the house. I'll be going now."), I got in my little red Volkswagen and started off towards the State Police substation in Elbridge. I struggled to suppress what I had just seen, thinking foolish thoughts about manliness and whether I would be seen as testosterone deficient if I betrayed what I was genuinely thinking and feeling. Mostly feeling. Trying to dim the horrifying image of the mother's shattered body, all I was left with was the echoing of the ominous question of why would a boy kill his mother? And in such a violent and gruesome way? And why did he place her in the bathtub? To avoid making a mess he knew she'd be unhappy about? I couldn't get my mind around it. I was calmer but not any better enlightened by the time I reached the substation around 3:30 in the morning.

The Elbridge State Police Substation was curiously placed at the end of a modest strip mall just on the village limits. It seemed old and it had an uncarpeted wooden floor. As I entered, I found Norm Mordue sitting on a desk in the front room, in serious and quiet conversation with a middle-aged man with graying sandy hair and wearing a tweed jacket. The man was awkwardly seated on a folding chair and his right foot was in a heavy plaster cast, propped up on a small stool. Also seated in the small office was D. Paige Gorham, a Falstaffian fellow of ample girth and appetite whose main achievement in life, besides being a lawyer of modest talent, was serving as the Town Justice.

Norm acknowledged my arrival with a nod but continued his conversation with the sandy-haired guy whose foot was in a cast. He was Frank Durgin, M.D., a well-known practicing psychiatrist at the V.A. and someone who was generally available to consult on forensic psychiatric matters for either the prosecution or the defense (but mostly the prosecution). His consultations were generally during normal business hours but because it was Senior Assistant District Attorney Norm Mordue calling about an urgent and interesting matter at two o'clock in the morning, Frank Durgin hoisted himself and his plaster cast out of bed and made his way out to this small police substation on the western edge of the County.

Norm was explaining to Durgin what the mission was. And it seemed pretty simple. Norm wanted Durgin to talk to the boy and assess whether he was suffering from a mental disease or defect. And then, if he was, to tell us whether, as a result of that mental disease or defect, the kid lacked a substantial capacity to know or appreciate the nature and consequences of his conduct or that such conduct was wrong. What Norm was asking Durgin to do was to anticipate any "insanity defense" the kid's lawyer might raise and to render his opinion as close in time as he possibly could to the act in question.

Now remember, I was a young lawyer at the time and the lawyer part of my brain understood, as Durgin understood, exactly what Mordue was saying and exactly what the purpose of a timely psychiatric assessment in this case would be. Norm was using the terms of New York's insanity defense law, as it existed at that time (it was substantially amended five years later) to detail to Durgin what he wanted him to do. But the non-lawyer part of my brain, the part that had just come from a ghastly scene and viewed a shattered woman's body lying in a blood-drenched bathtub was asking "What are you talking about? How can anybody do what this kid had just done and not know that he was shooting his mother? He marched her down a hall and made her stand in the bathtub and then blasted her full in the face. And shot her again. And how in the world could he or anybody not know that that was wrong?" I was tactful enough not to ask these questions and smart enough to simply shut up. I was there to learn, and I wouldn't any more think of interfering with Norm Mordue at work than I would ask questions of Sgt. Dick Sparrow.

What Norm had done really was brilliant. He was getting a psychiatric examination of the shooter within just a few hours of the crime, if it was a crime, and he wasn't waiting to get a Court ordered exam three months later. It was as if Ronald Regan was on his way to the hospital with a gunshot wound in his chest and his attempted assassin John Hinckley was being examined by a psychiatrist at the same time in the same hospital. If Durgin found that the kid essentially knew what he was doing, or that he knew that what he was doing was wrong, it was pretty much game, set, match for the prosecution. If, on the other hand, Durgin thought that the boy lacked the substantial capacity to know and understand these things, Norm wasn't going to waste prosecutorial resources to work towards a murder conviction which would likely be an unjust result even if successful.

Just as Norm wrapped up with Durgin, Investigator Milt White, who had been talking with the boy in a room at the back of the station, came in. I had known White as a short, rather intense guy, and the effect of spending the last couple of hours in a small closed room with a boy who had just shotgunned his mother to death was obvious. Radiating a sadness but also a grim determination, White silently walked over to a desk with a typewriter and continued the notes he had been progressively entering since his involvement earlier that night.

The boy had signed off on his "Miranda Rights," a deceptively simple one-sheet form with a series of check boxes for a suspect's initials where, in a one-stop shopping kind of way, the accused can scribble away a handful of Constitutional rights which the Founding Fathers had actually thought might come in handy in the event a citizen found himself in a small room and being asked questions by a guy with a gun, a badge, a set of handcuffs, and a notepad. Like the right to have an attorney. The right to shut up. The right to get up and leave if you weren't under arrest. You know, the usual, standard stuff. Just check and initial the boxes so we can talk. That gonna be alright? And your seventeenth birthday is when, again? The kid had waived his rights and, between tears, had talked to White about what had happened. Like maybe the end of his life as he thought he was going to live it. But he was talking, and that was something. White was putting the final touches on the kid's statement, the one that he agreed to sign.

Durgin hoisted himself up from his chair and with the aid of a cane started slowly hobbling back down the hallway to the room where the boy was. Tap, clunk-thump. Pause. Tap, clunk-thump. Pause. Tap, clunk-thump.

We sat in silence in the small front office. It was now about 4:00 a.m. Norm had gotten briefed by White as the questioning of the boy progressed, so he really didn't want or need any further information. Norm asked me if Sparrow had arrived. He then asked me if I had gone into the house and seen the body.

Momentarily unsure of what the right answer was (clearly, my doing so had displeased Sparrow), I told Norm that yes, I had gone in, had seen the gun, the groceries, the keys and the body and it was bloody and grim. Sensing my discomfort, Norm just nodded and didn't ask me for any more details (he would be getting the photos and forensics later in the day anyway). We then drifted off to small talk, White in the corner typing out a felony complaint charging the boy with Murder in the 2nd Degree. We sat waiting for Durgin to return.

4:00 a.m. became 4:15, then 4:45, then 5:30. The silver-gray uncertainty of early morning light came through the front and side windows. Still no Durgin. What could be taking so long? Was this really that complicated? We sat mostly in silence.

And then, after about two hours, we heard a door open, then close, then Clunk-thump. Pause. Tap, clunk-thump. Pause. Tap, clunk-thump.

When Durgin came in, he said nothing, but his affect mirrored White's when he came in earlier, a sadness and a grim frustration.

He sat down and stared at the floor for a few seconds, resting his hand on his upright cane.

Norm said, "So, Frank, whaddya think?"

A little more silence.

"This boy..."

Long pause.

I'm thinking, Yes, Frank? We're all thinking Yes, Frank?

We're all leaning in towards Durgin.

"This boy..."

Another long pause, longer than the first one.

We're all leaning in even closer.

"This boy has had...issues with his mother."

Bingo! There you go. Jeez!, I'm thinking, this is a real shocker. I never would have thought this! Boy am I glad we got a psychiatrist in on this early.

"She pushed him, and pushed him, and pushed him until he says couldn't take it anymore."

Norm hesitates, and then says,

"Did you reach an opinion, Frank? Did he know what he was doing? Did he know it was wrong?"

And Durgin says,

"Really Norm, I gotta think about it. Give me a couple of days."

Norm is deflated but has too much respect for Durgin to

either be annoyed or to press him on it. He'll just have to wait until Durgin thinks about it some more. At least he's gotten the benefit of a nearly contemporaneous psych exam, and that was something. And he's gotten an accurate read on the kid's emotional state.

Everybody leans back.

White gets up abruptly. He's holding the boy's confession, his Miranda Rights waiver form, and a felony complaint charging the kid with Murder. He's keeping the originals and has made three copies of each, sets for Norm, the Judge, and the kid. I don't get a set. He says, "You ready to arraign him Paige?" And that being the sole purpose for Judge Gorham to have been sitting there in the first place all night and early morning, D. Paige Gorham nods yes. White is about to leave to get the boy. Norm tells White to hold up. He spends a few minutes thinking.

Norm says, "Manslaughter. We're gonna charge Man 1." He turns to White and says, "Charge it up as extreme emotional disturbance." White seems just a little deflated, but he knows it's Norm's call so sits back down at the desk.

Cops tend to be black and white kinds of people. They usually see suspected criminality in pretty stark terms and are inclined to lodge the most serious charge they can think of given the circumstances they are presented with. Part of this is due to the understandable desire to be the one known for "cracking the big case" but it's also a function of their constantly finding serious criminality in the dark recesses of the world. For most of us, it's a headline of some awful kind of crime that shocks us; for many cops, it's depressing and an everyday thing. So, it was understandable that NYSP BCI Investigator Milt White saw this case as a Murder and he was, accordingly, busy drafting a felony complaint charging the kid with the most serious crime there is.

But Norm saw it differently. Not that he could ever be accused of being a "bleeding heart" or "soft on crime", but if there was one thing that Norm Mordue was about it was doing the right thing. And after spending all of the weary early morning hours in that NYSP substation, listening to the reported events, getting updates from White, and, especially, thinking about Dr. Durgin's description of the boy's emotional state and Durgin's hesitancy in pronouncing the boy insane or suffering from a mental disease or defect, Norm instinctively knew that as terrible a crime as this was, it really didn't neatly fit as a murder. Yes, it was horrific, and yes the boy had taken several steps to intentionally blast his mother into oblivion; but still, Norm was bothered by the same thought I had had when I was driving over to the substation: what could bring this kid to a point that he would do such a thing?

From what little Durgin did say, it was pretty clear that the boy felt driven to it. To Norm, this wasn't a murder, it was manslaughter in the first degree. If things changed over the next few days or weeks, or other proof emerged, the charge could still be upgraded to Murder 2. For now, we were going to go with Man 1 and he instructed White to draft the felony complaint accordingly. White did what he was told.

Of course the difference between murder and this particular type of manslaughter is a distinction without a difference as far as the dead person is concerned. But under the law in New York they are very different crimes. Basically, a murder is the intentional taking of another person's life and the penalty upon conviction is life in prison. But when the act of murder is committed under circumstances which likely show the actor was acting, at the time, under the influence of what the law calls an "extreme emotional disturbance", the crime is reduced to the level of Manslaughter in the 1st Degree, punishable by a max of 25 years, not life. Think of what used to be called "in the heat of passion." A guy comes home to find his best friend in bed with his wife and he reacts by shooting his best friend to death in the bed. Manslaughter. Same guy finds the best friend in bed with his wife, the best friend gets dressed and leaves, and the guy shoots the friend to death a week later because he's still hot about it. Murder. The difference has to do with the emotional circumstances, the timing of the conduct, and whether the actor really had time to rationally deliberate over it.

White finishes the revised felony complaint, this time using the same facts but charging the lesser offense of Man 1, extreme emotional disturbance. He makes another three sets (again not a set for me), gives Norm a chance to read it and be satisfied (which he is). Norm nods, White leaves to get the kid.

Norm hands me his copy of the statement and complaint and I move to the side of the room, leaning against the paneled wall. I'm reading the papers when I sense a stirring close to my right. Very close. It's the boy. He's maybe 5'6", 125 pounds tops. He has longish sandy blonde hair, a cluster of which falls down across his eyebrows. He's wearing a cream and blue striped tee shirt and chinos. And he is very very pale, his lips strangely a light purple. He is literally quivering. It's not cold in the room; in fact, there's a dank warm humidity which has accumulated over all the early morning hours when several large men gathered to discuss terrible things. So, the boy wasn't cold. He was just frightened to death.

D. Paige Gorham is seated four feet in front of the boy, going through the ritualistic incantations of a criminal arraignment, reading the charge, explaining his limited rights, but the boy's not there. He says nothing. He's alone on a catatonic journey to an empty plateau on another planet, and if he has any thought at all in his head it's one that is telling him he's never coming back. I'm not listening to Paige either. I'm staring at the boy, the steel handcuffs manacling his thin wrists, and, to my shock, the steel leg irons the troopers have affixed to his ankles. Really? Chaining his legs? Where's he going? There are five adult men surrounding him in a small closed room and the likelihood of his bounding out and through the parking lot of the strip mall at six o'clock in the morning is as unlikely as the rest of us breaking into a whistling version of "Sweet Georgia Brown."

It only takes a few minutes to arraign the boy. He is then escorted out and into a blue and yellow NYSP cruiser and taken to downtown Syracuse to be booked into the Public Safety Building, a venerable multi-tiered concrete and steel jail fortress which radiated indifference to each and every tragic story being lived by each and every inmate.

Sobered, tired, and drained by the night's events, I excuse myself and head home in my little red VW, a warm and loving home, to enjoy a hot breakfast. On the ride back, I can't help but be feeling that it would be a very long time, if ever, that the kid would be able to do the same thing.

That was 40 years ago. Since then, I have witnessed countless moments of heartbreak and drama played out in the criminal justice system. But the sight of the slight boy in handcuffs and steel leg irons shivering in the early morning light in that small office in the police station has never left me. Murder has many victims.

"DOES YOUR DOG BITE?"
"NO, BUT I DO."

If your major objective in applying to law school is to make a lot of money, you've probably made the wrong career move. You want to get rich? Become a hedge fund manager or design a new meme for Sonic the Hedgehog. I'm not against making money and I'd be a 24karat hypocrite to criticize lawyers who make serious money practicing law. But it's not why I became a lawyer. I've gotten a whole lot more satisfaction in helping people in need who are without resources to hire a lawyer than in sending out a large but well-earned bill to a client with means but whose life would go on swimmingly if their case didn't turn out the way they wanted. Doing true pro bono work is a sign you are a professional. It also qualifies you not to tolerate people who tell those lame lawyer jokes.

Sometimes doing pro bono work presents you with an opportunity to be exposed to a new area of the law, someplace you wouldn't ordinarily venture into. Like Social Security Disability. Let me be frank here: if I had to do only Social Security Disability cases for the rest of my career, I'd shoot myself. But there was one time I took on a disability case and it was a "learning experience" in every sense of the word.

I got a call from my friend Joe Lamendola, a really excellent guy, looking for my help. Joe was a lawyer, a retired Lieutenant Colonel with the Air National Guard, and he had volunteered to head up the Veteran's Law Clinic at Syracuse University's College of Law. Joe was deservedly well-liked and highly respected (he's now a State Supreme Court Judge) and it was never easy to say no to him when he called for an ask.

Joe tells me that the Veteran's Clinic is looking for a lawyer to help a disabled Marine who has been turned down in her application for Social Security disability. I tell Joe that I have as much experience in Social Security Law as I do in repairing NASA rockets and I'm not sure I could be of any real help. He responds, of course, with flattery, telling me that I'm a smart guy, I could get up to speed on this stuff in no time at all, that doing a hearing like this wouldn't be any different than the countless hearings I've done in the past, yadda, yadda, yadda. I relent, of course (flattery goes a very long way with me), and tell Joe I'll help. I ask him to send me the file.

I get the file, which is surprisingly thick. A bigger surprise to me is why the client, we'll call her Felicia, was turned down for disability benefits from the Social Security Administration in the first place. She's 23 years old, had served a combat tour in Iraq, had suffered a fractured ankle and a broken back, and was diagnosed with fairly severe PTSD. The V.A. had granted her an 80% disability (which was raised to 90% and then 100% during the relatively short time I represented her). My first reaction, one that never left me, was how on earth can anyone say she's not "disabled"? Well, I found out that there's a long answer to that question.

The V.A., which last I checked is just another branch of the same Government which operates the Social Security Administration, has her nearly totally disabled but apparently the SSA didn't get the memo. I'm thinking the world of SSD has got to be a strange one. Little did I know.

So, I get out a few books and do some on-line research and gear up to do an administrative SSD hearing and the deeper I go the more of a puzzle this stuff is to me. I made a commitment, of course, and I want to help, but this is going to be somewhat of a challenge.

What I learn is that each agency has its own measure of "disability" and a person's employability is a significant factor as far as Social Security is concerned. I'm sure some analyst somewhere deep in the bowels of the SSA is working full-time to expose those freeloaders who might have wangled a 100% disability rating from the V.A. but are still able to work part time and go bowling on Monday nights.

I'm trying to figure this stuff out with books and research, but I decide I need to meet with the client. I reach out to Felicia and ask her to come in for an initial client conference. I meet her in the waiting area of my office suite and from the get-go we're not off to a great start.

"Felicia? I'm Ed. Nice to meet you soldier." I put my hand out.

She rises and firmly takes my hand but says, "I'm not a soldier, I'm a Marine."

Oooookay. Noted.

Felicia is, at most, 5'2", a wiry 120 pounds, and though cordial she radiates intensity. As she gets up from the sofa, I realize she is accompanied by a dog, a small dark brown and blonde long-haired mix with the intense focus of a border collie beading in on a small clutch of nervous sheep. Felicia is all business. The dog is all business. We go back to my office. Felicia sits down and the dog (her name is "Cuse") curls up at her feet. The dog keeps staring at me, checking me out for a false move, not in any menacing way but with a sustained focus which is just a tad unnerving. And I like dogs.

Since I'd familiarized myself pretty thoroughly with Felicia's medical records, I don't spend a lot of time exploring the nature of her physical disabilities. The fractured back and ankle were the results of an overturned jeep accident and those injuries spoke for themselves. She occasionally required a cane to get around. Her PTSD had a pretty dramatic and shocking origin and I saw no need to explore it much except to have her tell me that Cuse was part of her prescribed therapy, that Cuse was a highly trained and certified service dog, and that Felicia actually had to get a prescription to obtain the animal.

Despite the "I'm not a soldier, I'm a Marine" opening, I'm finding that Felicia is pleasant and straightforward, but there's not a lot of humor flowing outbound. I also realize, after about 5 minutes of conversation with her, that there's something off. It's indefinable except to say it's definitely there, a form of hypervigilance that probably is not going to detonate while she sits there. But that's a probably.

Felicia explains to me the difficulties she's had holding jobs, even ones that don't challenge her intellect: desk clerk at a hotel, housekeeping. Her ability to lift 10 pounds is very limited, she can't stand erect for a sustained period of time, and she has difficulties concentrating on even simple tasks. Her Vocational Assessment record from the V.A. file corroborates everything she's telling me.

I take as many notes as I can and I'm hoping I can get a vocational rehabilitation expert to volunteer me some time to figure out what the best approach might be with Social Security. We spend about an hour together. An hour. The dog doesn't move, doesn't blink, but it's like she's listening as intently as the client. We finish up by my telling her what to expect at the hearing in two weeks (never having done one, I'm a real expert, of course) and Felicia and Cuse leave.

My next step is to get a rehab expert who knows something about the arcane world of Social Security disability. If it were a forensic problem involving muzzle velocity of a Ruger 9mm pistol, I'd have a fat Rolodex of qualified experts to consult with. But vocational rehab's not really in my wheelhouse so I reach out to my long-time friend Dr. Ken Reagles, the former chair of Syracuse University's Department of Rehabilitation Services. Ken's a super guy, a killer golfer, and early in his career he was a consultant to the Israeli Defense Force on the problems of veterans with PTSD. Perfect. Except Ken is traveling on business for the month so he refers me to one of his younger colleagues, Karen Simone, a young woman with a world of experience in rehab classifications. Karen is not only smart, she's generous and willing to help without charging a fee. Once again, my mother's wisdom (the lodestar of my life) is validated: it always pays to be nice to people.

With Karen's help, my several hours of research, and a close reading of Felicia's entire V.A. record, I put together a brief for the SSA Judge (her name is the Hon. Marie Greener), a submission which makes it appear that I know what I'm doing and that this is an open and shut case. Such is the bravado of naivete. Even lawyers suffer from it.

On the appointed day at the appointed hour, Felicia, the dog, and I find our way over to the Social Security Administration's Hearing Suite in a nearby office building. I've got the file, I've got the client, I'm imbued with the naïve confidence that Felicia's disability is so plain that we/she cannot be denied. We sign in at the entrance. That's me, Felicia, and the dog. Cuse doesn't have to sign in. We're sitting there for maybe 15 minutes when this guy comes out, identifies himself as Judge Greener's clerk, and tells me that the Judge would like to see me before we start. Just me. Not the client.

By this point in my career I've probably had well over 100 trials (mostly criminal) and somewhere in the neighborhood of 400-500 pretrial conferences or hearings, so even though I'm in a somewhat strange, and definitely new, environment, I don't regard this summoning to chambers as all that unusual. Except it's not to chambers. I'm directed to the courtroom.

Sitting there, resplendent in the full robe and jabot ensemble is Judge Greener. She greets me in a somewhat distant, businesslike fashion. As the dialogue enfolds, I find I'm sliding slowly into a fog of unreality that becomes stranger by the minute. It starts out pretty simply.

"Good morning counselor. I wasn't expecting to see a lawyer on this case. You didn't file a Form SSA-1696 or a 1699."

"Yes, good morning Your Honor. I'm appearing as a pro bono volunteer through the S.U. College of Law's Veteran's Clinic. I'm sorry, I haven't done one of these before and I'm not familiar with these forms."

"Well, it's basically you have to file a Notice of

Representation and a Request for a Fee and they have to be signed by the client. You haven't done that."

She helpfully hands me the forms.

"Well, I'm not asking for a fee here. I'm doing this pro bono."

"Okay, but you still have to fill these out and have your client sign them."

"Yes, Your Honor. I'll take care of that right now."

I start to turn away. But there's something else on her mind.

"Will you be requesting an adjournment here?"

"An adjournment? No, I don't think so. I think I'm familiar with the record and I've submitted a hearing brief."

"Yes, I've read your brief. Very nice. But since it appears you haven't done one of these cases before, there are some issues here you might not have thought about."

Judge Greener then lays out three procedural twists in the history of the case (unbeknownst to me, Felicia had applied for benefits a year earlier but then withdrew the application), twists I in fact hadn't thought much about; but none of them were things I couldn't handle off the top of my head.

"No, thank you. I don't think we'll need an adjournment. My client's been waiting weeks for this hearing already. I think we're prepared to go forward today."

I again turn away, my file in one hand the SSA forms in the other.

But there's something else on her mind. The real reason she called me in.

"There's just one more thing. No dogs."

"Excuse me?"

"I see your client brought along her dog. I don't allow

dogs in my courtroom."

"Judge, this dog is not a pet or a companion animal. It's a service dog. My client has been diagnosed with PTSD and the dog is part of her prescribed support therapy. The dog is highly trained and certified as a service animal."

"I don't care if it's Rin Tin Tin, the dog's not coming into my courtroom. You wouldn't believe what some applicants try and bring in here. Last week I had a woman ask if she could bring in her pony to the hearing. You're going to have to make other arrangements."

"Judge, she can't leave the dog in the waiting room."

"Go talk to your client. Tell me what she wants to do."

I'm thinking, no, this can't be right. Granted, I'm a stranger in a strange land here and Social Security Disability law is probably even stranger than I initially supposed it to be when I tried to beg off Joe Lamendola's request to take this on. But it can't be that complicated; it can't be at odds with fairness and common sense. This is a disability hearing, right? My Marine has a disability. The doctor who is treating her PTSD says she needs the service dog to help her cope with her disability. Shouldn't be complicated. Instinctively, I'm thinking that Judge Greener is on the wrong side of this proposition, but it would be foolish to stand there and argue with her without having some law to back me up. So I realize I'm going to need a little more time.

In the one minute it takes me to go from the courtroom to meet with my Marine and the dog in the waiting area, I consider the best way to explain the situation to Felicia. I opt for the approach direct. She's sitting on a small couch with Cuse curled at her feet. I pull up a chair so we can talk quietly and we are nearly head to head.

"She won't let you have the dog in the courtroom."

My Marine considers this for a few seconds.

"The woman's a fucking idiot. And she's the one who's gonna judge my case?"

"She's wrong. Let me handle it."

Our client conference is over. I know what I'm going to do. I give Felicia the two forms to sign and return to Judge Greener's courtroom.

"OK, counsel, what's it going to be?"

"Judge," I'm handing her clerk the signed forms, "With all due respect (a sure sign of code phraseology which Judges immediately recognize that the respect that's forthcoming is likely to be minimal at best), I think your policy is in error and my client has the right to have her service dog with her in the hearing." I continue on without giving the Judge a chance to respond. "I'd like to brief the issue for you. Can we get a short adjournment so I can put together a submission for you to consider?"

Given the fact she offered me an adjournment even before the dog issue came up, she really had no choice. But she's surprisingly cordial and responds, "Sure, that won't be a problem. You can submit what you want, but that's been my policy." The "You can submit what you want", however, was her code and smoke signal to me that "Mister, you're way out of line here and you ought to stick with what you know how to do." She gives me a date three weeks out.

I return to Felicia and the temporarily exiled Cuse and explain that I'm going to file a brief with the Judge to show her she's wrong, telling my Marine "I got this." Felicia seems to have confidence in me (can't speak for the dog) but is not happy we have to wait another three weeks. We trundle off in the direction of my office, Felicia to drive home, me to do some research.

The research I do leads me to what is for me a pretty arcane legal area, the Americans With Disabilities Act and a bunch of Federal regulations. But it takes me less than an hour and I have what is, in my opinion, the definitive answer. The Judge's "policy" is not merely wrong; it is way out of line and in fact illegal.

Since Cuse is a certified "service animal" which is defined by Federal regulation (a definition, by the way, which does not exclude ponies), I find out that "Individuals with disabilities shall be permitted to be accompanied by their service animals in all areas of a public entity's facilities where members of the public, participants in services, programs or activities, or invitees, as relevant, are allowed to go." Since Judge Greener's courtroom is a "public entity facility" and my Marine is a "participant in services" it would be a clear violation of the ADA to bar the dog from the hearing courtroom.

I write a tactful but forceful annotated two-page single-spaced letter to the Judge and file it with the court. It's less than a half a day's work. My initial commitment to Joe to "help out on a simple pro bono matter" in an area of law which is new to me has now turned into a situation I'm more familiar with: the contest of who's right? Me or the Judge? (I have built an entire career in firmly believing I'm right. It's one of my subspecialties.)

Two weeks go by. I don't hear from the Judge. We are two days out from the adjourned hearing date and still nothing. Felicia's calling me asking what's the story. Although it's never a good idea, in any venue, to call up a judge and ask if they've gotten around to deciding an issue in your case, I pick up the phone and call Judge Greener's chambers. I get one of her law clerks on the phone. She's a young woman, very cordial, and she tells me in a voice of barely suppressed elation as if I've just won the Publishers' Clearinghouse Sweepstakes that, yes, the Judge says Felicia can bring the dog in. Sweet victory! I call Felicia, deliver the good news, and tell her to meet me at the Social Security Hearing suite as scheduled.

Hearing day. I walk in, sign in, and see Felicia. I see Cuse. We're good to go. Although we are precisely on time, we sit there for more than a half an hour, then 45 minutes. Finally, the clerk who met with us the last time comes out, looking uncomfortable. I look up. Felicia looks up. Cuse looks up.

"Judge Greener won't be hearing your case today."

I ask, "Is there a reason?", suppressing my frustration and anger at knowing that there most assuredly is a reason. A reason of the canine variety.

He says, "Well, um, she's tied up." (Undoubtedly reviewing the minutes for her next ASPCA board meeting.) "We've made arrangements to have Judge Ramos hear your matter. It'll be another 20 minutes but we'll get you right in."

Felicia is giving me the here-we-go-again stare; Cuse is looking concerned. I'm without a response, especially since I know nothing at all about Judge Ramos and his views on service ponies, service squirrels, or service dogs. We wait in uncomfortable silence for the "Judge Ramos would like to see just you counselor" but that never comes.

Our case is called, we go into Judge Ramos' courtroom. With the dog. Ramos is friendly, professional, and well briefed. He's read everything I've filed and has reviewed the entire record. He asks Felicia a few questions, asks how old the dog is and tells us Cuse looks like his dog. He renders his decision in Felicia's favor from the bench, then and there (I learn later that most SSA Judges mail you their determination). He awards her every last penny she's entitled to and, given that the benefits are retroactive, that turns out to be a fair amount of money.

We leave Social Security, Felicia humming "From the Halls of Montezuma", Cuse showing me some tail wagging for the first time, and I'm feeling pretty good too. Like I said before, pro bono work's got some unexpected rewards. Those chances don't come too often. But I really should confess that I'm not sure what made me feel better: getting my Marine the SSD benefits she deserved or getting over on the Judge when she was wrong and I (thank you very much) was right.

ONE THROUGH THE HEART

From the beginning, it just didn't seem right to me. Not at all. I'm sitting in a neon-lit visitation cubicle facing an 18-year old boy charged with murder. His name is Aaron. There is no street swagger about him. He is handsome, unusually quiet, and polite. He has a beautiful ebony face above an athletic 6-foot build. He has immediate cred on the cellblock because he is charged with murder and his frame itself could signal to the other inmates that they should keep their distance. But there is no menace about him, and I can tell from his reaction to the noise in the cellblock that he is uncomfortable being here. Not, of course, just because it's a jail, and not because he is charged with the most serious crime there is, but because there is a constant voice in his head asking him how on earth he could have wound up here.

He had good reason to ask. His parents, Manny and Rose, were solid hard-working people who had raised Aaron and his siblings, his brother Nada (Nay-dah) and his sister Kizzie, to be respectful and generally obedient. They had their issues and challenges but who raises three teens without issues and challenges? The family had recently moved to Syracuse when Rose had a better opportunity with the telephone company and Manny found work doing maintenance for Lockheed Martin. Aaron chose to stay in Rochester for his senior year in high school, so he opted to live with his grandmother. It was a good choice for him; he was happy, and though he missed his family, things were working out for him. Until he bought a gun.

Even with his family in another city, Aaron felt generally secure. Mercifully, he had resisted the allure of joining one of the two street gangs in his neighborhood. But when he and a friend were threatened one day for doing little more than just walking down the wrong street, not aware that it was disputed territory warred over by the Hanna Street Posse and the DeJonge Street Crew, and then when another friend was murdered the next day, he felt the need for the added security of a handgun. What he bought (off someone on the street) was a cheap silver Titan .25 caliber semiautomatic pistol, a gun designed for close quarter encounters. If you needed a weapon to shoot something, say, three to four feet in front of you, this piece might hit it. At a longer range, it was simply a useless piece of junk. But still, it was a gun and it did give Aaron a small but wobbly sense of security.

The weekend was coming and Aaron wanted to see his family, so he took a very early morning bus from Rochester to Syracuse. Nada, who was 15, knew that his big brother was coming and he was excited to see him, so he invited his friend Neal Henry over. They both cut school so that they could spend time with Aaron. The three of them spent the morning doing what you'd expect young teens to do when they were cutting school: playing video games. Sometime during the morning, Aaron showed Nada and Neal the gun. It was a brief topic of discussion accompanied by a minor degree of awe and then forgotten about. They got back to playing video games.

In mid-afternoon, the three boys decided to go downtown, having no particular aim other than to just hang out. They were proceeding south on Salina Street when they encountered Terry Fulwiley, a 15-year old acquaintance of Nada's and Neal's. Some wise-ass words and taunting were exchanged and Neal and Terry started to wrestle and square off, accomplishing little other than having an annoyed adult intervene to break it up and tell them to move on. (Later, both boys characterized the scuffle as little more than horseplay but it certainly didn't appear that way at the time.) Aaron barked at both of them, stepped in, and sent Terry on his way. Terry stalked off south, in the direction of The Galleries, a downtown mall that had gone the way of similar properties, a lot of empty spaces and once chic storefronts now nearly vacant and available for rent.

Satisfied that Terry Fulwiley's annoyance had been eliminated, Aaron, Nada, and Neal continued their aimless stroll south on Salina Street. They had traveled a couple of blocks when they found themselves beneath one of the overhead street canopies at the Galleries. Out of the door came Terry Fulwiley. And Roger Fields. And Jay Hill. And the Flowers brothers. And Dynell Clark. And Yolanda Apples. And Kosmo Brown...and about 25 more black teens who had picked up on the rumor contagion coursing through the mall that there was going to be a fight. The crowd formed a swelling horseshoe around Aaron and the two boys, and Jay Hill, thinking he was Sugar Ray Leonard about to throw it down with Marvin Hagler, discarded his jacket and put up his dukes, egged on by the shouting of his homies. "Kick his ass!'

"We gonna mess you up motherfucka!" Aaron was not sure who all this was being directed at, but he realized they were in danger. So he did something that was both reasonable and foolish. He took out his gun.

Aaron was a large guy, and he had large hands. The small silver gun was not readily apparent as he held it, but he lifted his arm straight up in the air and fired it into the ceiling of the overhang canopy. The pop-bang of the small firearm had its intended effect, but only momentarily. The mob of startled teens took a half-step back, but none of them retreated. One of them shouted, "Tha's bullshit. It a cap gun! Get 'em!"

With that, Aaron wheeled, telling Nada and Neal to run, and the three of them took off, running north on Salina Street. The mob of teens took right off after them, yelling threats and apparently just getting off on the excitement of the chase. When Aaron and the two boys reached the first corner, they ran right, having no idea where they were or where they were going. Their aim, of course, was simply to get away. The scattered crowd of braying teens strung out along East Jefferson Street, a long block which ran along the side of the Cathedral of the Immaculate Conception and then opened widely into a fountained plaza which fronted the Onondaga County courthouse. Still not knowing exactly where he was, and having no plan other than to just get away, Aaron found himself at the curb of the sidewalk between the Courthouse and the Civic Center, a tall building immediately to the east. He turned and saw his scattered pursuers still crossing the fountain plaza, a boy named Roger Fields in the lead. Although only 14, Roger Fields was six feet one inch tall and weighed over 150 pounds.

Fearing the oncoming crowd, Aaron turned and fired his

gun twice. They were random shots and his only purpose was to slow and startle his pursuers, just as he had done on the Salina Street sidewalk three blocks away and moments before. Wherever one of the .25 caliber bullets landed didn't matter; but the other found its way dead center into the heart of Roger Fields who collapsed next to a trash can near the fountain. A six foot 14-year-old child, barely a teenager, lay dead on the sidewalk before the Cathedral fountain, just yards from the imposing Beaux Arts temple of the Onondaga County Courthouse.

At first Aaron had no idea that anyone had been hit or injured. He simply continued to run, along with Nada and Neal, through the mouth of the downtown building canyon, across the open plaza of the Everson Museum and the surrounding acres of parking lots, and finally under the I-81 highway overpass, about three quarters of a mile from where the shooting took place. He heard sirens in the far distance, but he was in a hospital area and it could have been ambulances.

He was under the I-81 overpass when a Syracuse police cruiser glided up. Officer Dan Whittles rolled down his window and asked the boys to stop. They scattered and ran, Aaron crossing behind the cruiser. Whittles got out of the car and took off after Aaron, calling for him to stop. Which he did. Whittles asked Aaron what he was running from and Aaron responded that there was some trouble downtown and he was trying to get away from it. Patting him down, Whittles found only a portable CD player and then asked Aaron to get into the back of the cruiser, something he did without protest. Two other SPD officers chased down the other boys and then the three of them were transported to the Criminal

Investigation offices to get the situation sorted out.

Which didn't take long. Nada and Neal were but 15 and although they knew they really hadn't done anything wrong (or at least not criminal), they were quite scared and pretty freely recounted what had happened. The police were rapidly gathering facts and witness stories and waited a good long while before they even spoke to Aaron. While Aaron sat and worried in a small windowless interrogation room, two officers returned to the grassy sidewalk where Whittles had intercepted Aaron and in pretty short order recovered the Titan .25 Aaron had tossed away.

Aaron had spent the haunting solitary hours in the interrogation room thinking about not just the next few hours, or even the next few days, but how the rest of his life had taken such a grim turn and how his whole world had changed forever. He knew that being left alone in this room for a long time was not a good sign. He was startled when Captain Dick Walsh came in and just stood over him, staring silently.

Walsh was a big guy with an imposing presence and his silent looming over Aaron was very unsettling. Walsh had been on the job a long time; he instinctively recognized that this kid was not a gangbanger. But he also had a dead 14-year-old lying on the pavement right in front of the courthouse. He lifted a small clear evidence bag containing the Titan .25 and showed it to Aaron. He simply said, "Son, you're gonna be charged with murder." Aaron looked at Walsh in sorrow and a few minutes passed. Fighting off unmanly tears, he finally said, "I didn't mean to kill him. I just shot at him. I could have shot when I was close."

I met with Aaron at the jail the next morning.

Indictment

It didn't take long for the Grand Jury to return an Indictment against Aaron. It was only two counts, but either one led up a ramp towards a steel door that once slammed shut by a conviction would doom what was still left of his young life.

There were two charges: Murder in the Second Degree (25 to life) and Criminal Possession of a Weapon in the Second Degree (15 years). Dark as that picture was, I pretty quickly sensed the outlines of a defense beneath the grim surface. Aaron wasn't going to walk; he clearly shot the boy. But there's murder, and then there's murder.

Not to get too granular about it, but it is important to understand the prosecution theory of murder. You would think that a charge of murder would be pretty easy to understand. In most circumstances, a guy kills someone with the intention of killing him; that's your typical intentional murder charge. It requires proof that the defendant acted with an intent to kill. Remember that pretty much the only statement that Aaron made to the police was "I didn't mean to kill him. I just shot at him. I could have shot when I was close." Self-serving as that statement was, it was at least something to build on. And it had the added advantage of being true.

But in New York, and lots of other states, you can be guilty of murder even if you don't have an intention to kill. Let's say you recklessly point a loaded shotgun at someone and fire it towards him, not directly at him, intending to scare him. The guy gets hit and dies. Your act is "reckless", not intentional, and that reckless act would ordinarily earn you a charge of Manslaughter in the Second Degree (recklessly causing the death of another person). The difference is important: Murder in the Second Degree is a Class A felony punishable by 25 to life; Manslaughter in the Second Degree, on the other hand, is a Class C felony with a max of 15 years. Obviously a big difference.

Change the scenario slightly: instead of one guy standing there, there's a group of ten standing together and even though you don't really intend to kill anybody, you fire into the crowd, killing one of them. The law would call this "depraved mind murder" ("Under circumstances evincing a depraved indifference to human life, [a person] recklessly engages in conduct which creates a grave risk of death to another person, and thereby causes the death of another person.") This elevates the seriousness of the crime to something which the law regards as an intentional act—murder.

The key to the prosecution proving depraved mind murder lies in the circumstances; were they so depraved and indifferent to the consequences that the actor may as well have intended to kill somebody? Take speeding at 80 miles an hour. If it's on a highway, you get a ticket. But what if that car is going in the wrong direction down a closed one-way city street and plows into a block party of neighbors? Does it really make a difference that the driver says, "I didn't mean to kill anyone"? Well, he did kill someone and the law will hold him accountable for murder. It's not his state of mind or intention that counts as much as the circumstances. I thought the circumstances of Aaron's act would, at least, militate against murder and that we would have a chance at the lesser crime of Manslaughter in the Second Degree.

I thought we had an even better chance at defending the weapon possession charge. The prosecution had to prove that Aaron possessed an unlicensed gun, that it was loaded, and that it was operable. Surely a no-brainer for a first-year law student. But what made the charge Criminal Possession of a Weapon in the Second Degree (and not the significantly lesser offense of Third Degree) was that it had to be shown that he possessed the gun "with intent to use the same unlawfully against another person." Did he? Even discounting his denial to the police that he had no intention of killing Roger Fields, remember that when Aaron first took out the gun on Salina Street, he displayed it and fired it straight up in the air. If he had an intention to use the gun unlawfully against another person, would he have done that?

Despite the gravity of the charges, I thought we had something to work with.

The Two P.J.s

In a classic example of mixed karma, the case was assigned to Assistant DA Patrick J. Quinn to prosecute and Onondaga County Court Judge Patrick J. Cunningham to preside over. But for the fortuity of their first name and middle initial being the same, these two men had nothing in common.

I liked Pat Quinn an awful lot. He was a quiet, reasonable, and utterly professional prosecutor with a low-key manner and a careful approach to his cases. My view of him was somewhat skewed, I know, by the fact that he was my former student when I taught trial practice at Syracuse University's College of Law and he was the first student I ever gave an A to. I had followed his career ever since then and was pleased when he deservedly got hired as an Assistant DA. Every once in a while I would check in with him, and, because he was such a talented guy, I frequently encouraged him to start thinking about life after the DA's Office. I suggested he have something like a five-year plan. I started giving this mentoring advice after he was there three years. Then five. Then seven. After twelve, I gave up. He was happy doing what he was doing and notwithstanding my own finely honed subspecialty of telling people what is best for them, I was happy for him. I was even happier for myself when I drew Pat as an adversary in Aaron's case, not because I entertained the absurd notion that he would go in the tank for me but because I knew I'd be dealing with a professional of talent and integrity:

So that was the good news.

The other Patrick J.? That guy was a whole different story.

Onondaga County Court Judge Patrick J. Cunningham, who everyone knew as P.J., was an elfin Irishman with glasses, big teeth, and a chattering style that endeared him to many lawyers. For one thing, most people thought he was a funny guy with a quick wit. This was largely true until you came to the realization that almost all his so-called witticisms were at the expense of other people, particularly anybody who might be vulnerable and was in no position to strike back. Like, say, a black teenager standing helplessly in front of him awaiting sentencing.

He was also an inveterate gossip, "the eyes and ears of the world" as my friend Judge Burke called him, always eager to share the latest buzz which might be going around the courthouse. And if it wasn't current gossip yet, P.J. had no compunctions about starting a rumor if it had even a microgram of truth just so long as it made for a good story. And didn't involve him.

His pretrial conferences, which were supposed to be in-chambers opportunities to seriously and quietly discuss a possible disposition of a case with the assigned D.A, were usually tag team affairs with small clutches of lawyers either standing around or sitting on tables, each vying for even some few minutes to get in a word about their client or a deal that might be workable. P.J. was big on deals. If it roughly comported with the law (which is another way of saying it wasn't blatantly illegal) and it would be O.K. with Joe Six Pack on the street, that was fine with P.J. Except if he didn't like the lawyer. In that case, whatever the D.A. wanted was how it was gonna be.

My very first hour of my very first day as a young and wholly inexperienced assistant district attorney sent me to P.J.'s chambers on a bail reduction matter. Since P.J. was a County Court Judge, he had the authority to review and overrule the bail determinations of a host of lower courts. These kinds of proceedings are about as routine as things get (which was why it was my very first assignment), but if you are, let's say, a worried parent who can't make the $50,000 bail that some farmer who is a part-time town judge slapped on your kid because he was annoyed to be yanked out of bed at 2:00 a.m. to arraign a drunken 17-year old who mouthed off to him, or you are a well-retained lawyer whose client had an oversupply of unfortunate felony convictions in his past, getting bail reduced to a makeable amount is sort of a momentary big deal.

There's usually a little horse trading or, at a minimum, a weighing of equities that goes on and it's rare that a motion for reduced bail turns into a seriously contested matter. Either side could, in theory, appeal to an even higher court (the Appellate Division in Rochester) but at least there would be a record to review to assess whether the lower court's determination was reasonable. It's supposed to ultimately come down to the Constitutional right not to be held on excessive bail. And what's fair. Over the years, I came to accept it as a given that if the pleading lawyer was a friend of the presiding judge, that counted for more than something. As a defense attorney, I was as guilty as the next guy in playing the my-friend-the-judge card if it was playable.

But in this situation, I wasn't a defense lawyer playing the judge-buddy card. It was literally my debut appearance as a prosecutor, a bail review for a car dealer's kid who was found inside a suburban kitchen of a house that wasn't his at 2:00 a.m. Maybe there was some explanation which wasn't made clear enough to the arresting officer or the town judge; maybe the ski mask, screwdriver, and flashlight were items he routinely carried to help out neighbors whose garbage disposal was stuck at 2:00 a.m.; maybe he was just confused. Or, maybe the guy was a criminal committing a home burglary. Whatever the explanation, whatever the circumstance, the guy's lawyer had the chance to make a pitch to get the kid out of the can. And the way it was supposed to work is that the D.A. can also give the judge whatever reasons there may be to leave the bail where it is or even increase it. That's how the law was supposed to work back then. And, stupid me, in my fresh out of law school three-piece suit that morning, that's how I thought it was going to be.

My bad.

I walk into P.J.'s chambers (where I knew ahead of time all manner of business got conducted, especially bail reviews) and the conversation pretty much goes as follows:

P.J.: "Eddie! Great to see you! First day, huh? Whaddya got?"

Me: "Yeah, Judge, thanks. I'm here on a bail review for D'Amico."

P.J.: "D'Amico? Frankie's kid? Yeah, I took care of that already. I R.O.R.'d him."

There was a full menu of possible responses for me to choose from here. "What are you talking about?" would have probably been the right one but I was too naïve, too inexperienced, and too gob smacked for that to even occur to me. The judge had ordered the kid released on his own recognizance (or, in reality, his Dad's) without hearing from the D.A. (that would be me). Instead, I just stood there for a second or two in uncomfortable silence and considered the possible consequences of making an issue out of this. It was, after all, in the grand scheme of things, a really trivial matter and it wasn't as if P.J. had acted corruptly (always a possibility with him, but not this time) or had intended to diss me personally. It was just how things rolled with this judge and I prudently decided to just roll with it myself.

The incident really was no big deal and not worth dwelling on here except for my learning a valuable lesson in dealing with P.J.: his courtroom was a favor bank not very far removed from the insurance claims office he started out in as an adjuster trying to chisel down policy holders with fender benders.

P.J. achieved distinction early in his judicial career by coming within a one-vote whisker of being removed from office by the Court of Appeals for writing letters to a lower court judge telling him that he would never reverse his judgments, conduct which the dissenters on the Court of Appeals called "a perversion of the judicial process". But because he was such a fun guy, for an overly long time the local bar didn't hold any of that against him. I started out with P.J. from Day One from a position of mistrust, if not to say disrespect. For most of my career, I had tried very hard to avoid him if I possibly could.

But before you think that this story is a masked attempt to air some pretty petty grievances from long ago, consider this: there was a much darker side to P.J. Cunningham.

What really set him apart for me was this: it wasn't just that he was incompetent and unqualified, he was the most racist judge I ever appeared before. Hands down. His racism wasn't just mean-spirited and condescending; it was racism as entertainment and, what's worse, it was something he probably didn't think of as wrong or offensive. The stories about his racism were legion; that's shocking enough, but the even greater affront to justice is the number of lawyers who didn't report him. (And, sadly, that would include me. More about that later.)

One time he was conducting a murder trial of a black defendant and he took a break to preside over his daily calendar. The calendar was moving towards conclusion when P.J. announced to those assembled that he had to hurry up so that he could "get back to trying that little assassin." One of the jurors was seated in the courtroom. Someone had the courage and good sense to report this remark to the State Commission on Judicial Conduct, an august body who meant business and who at that point were already growing weary of dealing with him. While that complaint was pending, P.J. was heard to remark during one of his group pre-trials that

"Dominicans are great baseball players, but too many of them are drug dealers." That too got reported to the Commission.

My hopes for justice were dimmed when P.J. was assigned to preside over Aaron's case. But there was nothing I could do about it.

A Pretrial with P.J.

As I mentioned before, pretrial conferences in Judge Cunningham's court were chaotic affairs and even something as serious as a murder case would be treated as group entertainment if there were enough lawyers around. Luckily, this pretrial conference was just Pat Quinn, P.J., and me.

The D.A. offered to accept Aaron's guilty plea to Murder in the Second Degree in exchange for the minimum sentence of 15 to life. That was fine with P.J. I made it clear that this was a non-starter for us. The kid was 18 with no prior record. He shot back at the crowd chasing him in self-defense. At the mention of self-defense, P.J. interjected, "Self-defense? Eddie, this was an assassination! And it happened right in front of my courthouse! And I saw the whole thing through my window. You're going nowhere with self-defense."

I knew and Pat knew that P.J.'s chambers were on the north side of the building and since the shooting took place on the south side, well out of P.J.'s range of view, the only thing P.J. could have seen was a bunch of cops running by his window well after the shooting.

I briefly entertained the notion of getting P.J. to recuse himself because he was a witness, but I also realized that his claim of witnessing the shooting was a product of his dimly bordered imagination and would crumble under any serious analysis.

I also refrained for yet another reason, one that I thought I could eventually use to my advantage: by that time in my career, P.J. knew I saw through his petty meanness and bullshit and I was willing to stand up to him (sadly, that made me a member of a pretty small population). Though I didn't like dealing with him, he was, like most bullies who are actually cowards, pretty easily intimated and scuttled away like a land crab when confronted.

I still tried to convince Cunningham that the Indictment should be dismissed because the Grand Jury wasn't instructed on the law of self-defense, but he rejected that out of hand. I knew that "self-defense" wasn't applicable to the charge of Possession of a Weapon, but apparently being chased through city streets by a mob of teenagers yelling "We're gonna kick your ass" didn't impress the judge as much of a threat to the defendant's physical safety. I was convinced, however, that even the sneaky little racist he was would still instruct the jury by the end of the trial on the law of self-defense if for no other reason than that he was afraid of getting reversed after an appellate court looked at the facts. I should also add that despite our phony bonhomie from time to time, P.J. was afraid of me. Not physically of course; it's just that he thought I was too smart by half and would use every opportunity I could to embarrass him (which, I've got to say wasn't that hard; he was pretty stupid. His path to the bench was built on glad-handing at Republican clambakes and telling funny stories at VFW halls, two things he was very good at. It certainly had nothing to do with merit, legal ability, or judicial temperament).

As things progressed, I tried to be careful about crossing over from principled and firm opposition to clear disrespect, but it wasn't terribly easy. There was the time I insisted on getting a weather report into evidence (it was admissible by statute) and P.J.'s response was:

> It's not coming in and it's now five of twelve and if we stay here until two o'clock this morning and you keep talking, and I know you're trying to make a record and make me look bad because the judge is holding out this vital information, it's absolutely absurd. It is not going to go in and I can give you another ten minutes or something.

Well, I did just keep talking. And, yes, I was trying to make him look bad. And he knew it. But he still gave me ten more minutes. It didn't come in. But that wasn't the point. If there was one thing he knew for certain it was that he couldn't screw with me. I was no longer the fresh-faced A.D.A. in a freshly pressed suit on my first day on the job.

The pretrial, as expected, went nowhere. But P.J. knew I intended to press self-defense and that we were not going to roll over.

The Big Picture

I knew right away that the key to defending this case was the mob of kids who surrounded, threatened, and chased Aaron. If I could get the jury to see, feel, and hear what Aaron was experiencing as he was being chased down unfamiliar city streets, I thought the jury would have a more empathetic view of the case and view Aaron in a more understanding light.

And let me be perfectly candid and maybe cynically racist here: the fact that all of these kids were black increased the chances that the jury (which odds-on were likely to be mostly white) would see them as a threat (to anyone, but especially to the jurors themselves). From the police reports and interviews (and there were many) I had names and addresses. And ages. There may have been as many as 30 of them, but not one was over 16 years old and most were 14 and 15. It would be a task and a half to find all of them much less interview them. And you didn't have to be an inner-city middle school teacher to understand that each of them would likely carry an attitude should they have to appear in a courtroom. (I was cynical enough to think that this too would help me. Which it did). I knew that the prosecution would be calling some of them, but as few as possible. They were witnesses, after all; but the D.A. did not want too many. They would all pretty much tell the same story. No need to remind the jury that they constituted a mob. I wanted all of them; or at least as many as we could track down.

I was lucky enough to have the assistance of my talented and industrious friend Joe Lucchesi who volunteered to "second chair" the case with me (and I was very grateful). Never having tried a felony case before– much less a murder – Joe wanted the trial experience (even though the Onondaga County Assigned Counsel System wasn't paying for a second lawyer in homicide cases in those days , Joe was eager to help). Joe was a very personable guy and I instinctively knew he would be perfect to track down most of the kids who chased Aaron, get additional statements if necessary, and put a trial subpoena in their hands. All of which he succeeded in doing with great determination and success.

I set about to see if I could find any witness who the police may have overlooked and who might turn out to be helpful. I had one particular guy in mind. I knew that the kids who chased Aaron streamed east along Jefferson Street and on the sidewalk closest to the Cathedral (which was on the south side of the street). There were a series of small storefronts on the north side of Jefferson and knew that one of them was a one-man tailor shop.

The man who owned it was a self-important Middle Eastern tailor who I knew spent most of his time at an ironing board and workstation which situated him with a direct view of Jefferson street. And the guy spent most of his time standing and facing the street. The pandemonium of the chase wouldn't have been just hard to miss; it would have been impossible to miss. He at first greeted me with all the obsequiousness he reserved for the lawyers and judges in the area and to whom he considered himself their personal haberdasher. But as soon as he realized I was defending the kid who loosed two shots in the fountain plaza down the block a couple of days before, his deference to me evaporated and he seemed to experience a memory loss on a level of cognitive impairment not yet known to medical science. Saw nothing, heard nothing, knew nothing. I really wouldn't have much minded if he honestly told me he just didn't want to get involved. He was just out and out lying and didn't want to help. Period. That was the last time I brought my trousers into him for hemming.

I had better success with another idea I had. Just after sunrise one morning, I drove down to the County Courthouse and mounted the very wide steps which cascaded down from the handsome set of doors which, though quite ornamental, had fallen out of use for a variety of reasons (mainly security). Mounting to the top of the steps in the quiet early morning, I was able to get a panoramic shot with my camera which captured the fountain plaza, the "scene of the crime", pretty much from the perspective I wanted the jury to view it. It perfectly captured the space that Aaron would have been looking at as he fled. In the post-dawn hours, of course, that space was quiet and quite empty.

I took the photo to Syracuse Blueprint who enlarged it on a 2' x 4' foamboard to use as a trial exhibit. My plan was to have each of the kid witnesses (my trial file labeled them as "chasers") put a green dot showing his or her location when they either saw or heard the shots fired. I anticipated that the large black and white poster photo would be festooned with a sea of small green dots by trial's end. I was not disappointed; by the end of the trial that's exactly what it looked like.

The Prosecutor's Tale

Every good trial lawyer knows that trial work is very similar to storytelling. You've got to tell the jury a story and it can't just be once-upon-a-time. It needs to be a story that captures the jury's interest and then holds on to it.

A murder case has a built-in interest, but you need to be careful in how you develop it. Starting your case with the right first witness is almost as important as laying out a compelling narrative in your opening statement. After living with the facts of your case for months, sometimes years, and knowing the story in minute detail, your brain can easily lose track of the fact that the jury is hearing all of this for the first time and they don't know anything you know. And how it comes out of the gate is a very reliable predictor of how it's going to look at the finish line. So starting with the right person who can establish the point of view you want is really important.

One time I was conscripted to act as a special prosecutor in a highly circumstantial murder case. We were convinced that the defendant murdered his wife at around 3:00 P.M. We theorized that he left his downtown business at around 2:30 in the afternoon, drove up to his nearby suburban home, continued his argument with his wife, and then killed her by knocking her out and drowning her in the bathtub. It would have taken him no more than 15 minutes to get home and no more than 10 or 15 minutes to kill her. He had a Home Depot receipt showing that he had returned a hammer at 3:34 and Home Depot was less than 10 minutes from his house. So there was a window, a narrow one, where he could have been home, done the deed, and then driven to the hardware store to establish an alibi.

We had a lot of proof against this guy—his background, his suspicious behavior, his motive (a big and totally unjustified insurance policy on his wife who didn't speak English and did not work outside the home)—and I had lots of options for how to start the story (acquiring the insurance policy, the wife's immigrant status, his efforts to flee the country) but most of those avenues of proof would have engendered vigorous cross-examination and early squabbles with his very accomplished and smart set of lawyers. I needed something which was definitive, important, and nearly incontestable. I started with a 15-year-old schoolgirl.

She didn't know the defendant or anyone connected with the case. But she did know one thing and, for me, it was literally a killer fact. She rode the school bus every day and the bus schedule had the bus passing the defendant's house between 2:55 and 3:10. She remembered seeing the defendant's car in the driveway when the bus passed around

3:00 P.M. the day before, which was the day of the murder. This was not as far-fetched as you might at first think. The defendant had but one car and it was a very distinctive car (a two-tone Cadillac Seville with a patterned brougham top) and the girl reported seeing the car when she was interviewed just one day after the murder. This was the result of utterly brilliant police work by the gifted detectives who were assigned to work with me: John Maslona, John Conroy, and Jim Corgel. The day after the homicide, they set up a roadblock on the busy street in front of the house and questioned motorists between 2:30 and 3:30 to see if anyone habitually came by the house during that time frame. Jackpot. The girl on the bus remembered the car in the driveway the day before and it had to have been in the narrow window we had posited for the murder.

So, I called her as my first witness. The crucial fact, practically undeniable (who's going to vigorously cross-examine and challenge a 15 year old girl who has no interest in the case?) was that the defendant was home at 3:00 o'clock, a fact which he had vigorously denied. It also made his Home Depot receipt totally irrelevant. As I expected, the lawyer's cross-examination went nowhere and the jury was starting out with a fact that never changed and was never challenged. The defendant was home at three o'clock. I wouldn't say that my first witness, the schoolgirl, determined the outcome of the case, but her testimony surely impacted the jury's view and the defense never recovered (the guy was convicted and sentenced to life in prison).

So, beginning with the right witness to start your story is important.

Nada

It was, therefore, a mild surprise to me that Pat called Aaron's brother, Nada as his first witness. There was a logic to it, of course. Nada was with Aaron the entire time, could put the gun in Aaron's hands, and he witnessed the shooting. On the other hand, none of those facts were really going to be contested and by calling Nada, Pat gave me an early opportunity to develop the fright the brothers were feeling when being chased by the mob of teenagers and also to bring out some positive things about Aaron since the brothers clearly loved each other and Aaron was acting, in part, to protect his younger brother.

Maybe Pat wasn't in class the day I was lecturing on the importance of your first trial witness; I wouldn't have started with Nada if I was prosecuting. I would have started with one of the many startled and frightened civilian witnesses milling about the cathedral fountain in front of the courthouse that day and who were scared to death by hearing and seeing gunshots in that busy downtown area. But Pat started out with Nada and followed with Neal Henry, both telling essentially the same story of street confrontation, chase, shots, and flight. It wasn't great for us, but I really didn't see how it set up the story the way Pat intended.

As if sensing that he might be starting off by giving the jury a point of view that seemed to favor the defense (Aaron, Nada, Neal), Pat pretty quickly shifted perspective and started in on the various witnesses to the shooting who were in and about the courthouse plaza. (This is not to criticize Pat; he was a sharp and effective prosecutor. It's just I would have done it differently.)

One Through the Heart

The jury then heard from a lady named Lisa Howard who had the misfortune to be sitting in a car which was double parked immediately adjacent to the Courthouse and Civic Center and was witness to Aaron turning to fire the gun, on the sidewalk and just a few feet to her left. It was, without question, important testimony and it was dramatic. But it was also skewed by the fact that she was facing south when Aaron stopped and fired towards the northwest, that she had no context or framework for what was going on or had immediately preceded it, she didn't know how far away Roger Fields was when he was hit, and she didn't see him getting hit. All she really knew or saw was that a tall black kid immediately to her left and outside the car suddenly let two shots fly.

The distance between the Fields kid and Aaron became a significant issue and we spent a good deal of back and forth over the question. Pat called Officer John Knittle, an evidence technician with the Syracuse Police Department. Knittle testified that he recovered two bullet casings (shells) along the curb line on Montgomery Street and that the distance from those ejected shells to the spot where Roger Fields fell was approximately 50 to 51 feet. This was probably the most reliable estimate of the distance, but over the course of the trial we had wildly conflicting witness estimates. Aaron himself put the distance at about 75 feet and one of the prosecution witnesses, 15-year old Quincy Goode, put the distance as a wholly improbable "eight or nine feet." The host of other teenagers called as witnesses estimated the distances, as best they could, between those two points, but at least the jury got a better understanding of what Aaron meant when he told the police that "I could have shot when I was close." He wasn't close.

My cross-examination of 15-year old Quincy Goode came at a point fairly late in the prosecution's case (Pat had already put on four other teens from the chasing group) and by then I had reached and exceeded my quota of inarticulate teenagers with an attitude. None of them were particularly reliable in the first place and I could sense that Pat knew it. (One of the witnesses, Larry Mays, aka "Big L", helpfully opined that the group of kids confronting Aaron and his brother numbered "53". How he reached that census estimate I couldn't tell you, but it didn't do much to bolster the prosecution's argument that self-defense didn't apply.)

In any case, I am all over Quincy Goode trying to get an intelligent answer to the question of where he was when he saw and heard Aaron shoot back at the crowd that was chasing him and how far he thought Aaron was from Roger Fields:

Q How close did you ever get to the gun during any of this?

A I don't know. I didn't have no ruler on me.

Q I can't hear you.

A I said, I do not know. I didn't have a ruler on me.

Q You didn't have a ruler on you?

A No.

Q Well, close enough to know it was a gun, right?

A Right.

Q All right. You're standing in front of that church and you see Aaron on the corner I'm sorry, in the street in front of the courthouse, is that your testimony?

A Um-hmm, yes.

Q And you didn't have a ruler there, did you? Do you

know how far that is from the church to the middle of the street?

A Well, back on Salina Street he raised the gun and we seen it.

Q Okay. But you didn't get a real good look at that gun when you were on the circle in front of the church, did you? You just heard it?

A I seen it.

Q You saw it because you recognized the color, isn't that right?

A Right.

Q And didn't you just tell Mr. Quinn you didn't get a real good chance to see the gun, other than the color?

A I can't tell you what kind of gun it was.

Q You couldn't? Are you familiar with guns?

A No.

MR. QUINN: Judge, will he let the witness answer.

THE COURT: He's fifteen years old, please.

The transcript of this interchange doesn't convey this kid's slouching body language and facial expressions, but at this point I'm not proud to say that my frustration had gotten the better of me and I'm raising my voice, nearly popping a cork. Pat was right to intervene. But the reason I'm quoting it at some length is to highlight P.J.'s admonishment "He's fifteen years old, please" which, of course, he said in front of the jury, showing them what a fair-minded guy he is, being sympathetic to the limitations of a young witness. OK. My bad. Not in the finest tradition of the bar.

But now young Quincy is off the stand and the jury has been dismissed for the day. I'm complaining to P.J. in a pretty loud voice (once again) that he had been inappropriately cutting me off all trial and besides that he was letting the D.A. ask too many leading questions. P.J. and I then really get into it and he finally says "My courtroom, my ruling, my discretion, and that's the way it's going to be, and how I'm going to run the trial" and he then leaves the bench. I have a few more minutes to cool off and I'm thinking maybe I went too far with him, so I find him in his chambers to sort of apologize. He acts as if nothing has happened and that he loves me like a nephew.

"Nah, that's all right Eddie. That little coon was giving you a hard time. These kids Pat's putting on, they're like a parade of little apes, aren't they?"

I should have said something. But I didn't. I had a trial to do. I just left. Why bother with this guy?

Parade of little apes or not, we were determined to have the jury get a forceful sense of the mob of kids in the chase, so when it was our turn we called six more of them (Dynell Clark, Jay Hill, Erik Flowers, Emanuel Flowers, Yolanda Apples, and Dorothy Murray). I really didn't care about whatever they said (the story from the Galleries to the plaza never really changed no matter who was telling it); what I did care about was what they were (a mob) and where they were. I had Joe Lucchesi handle the questioning of these kids (prudently limiting my own opportunity to once more pop a cork and lose control; in any case Joe is the one who had tracked them down prior to trial). What was really important, and what we succeeded in doing, was to fill the enlarged poster board photo of the fountain plaza with a sea of green dots (each kid dutifully marked where they were) so that the jury had a clear picture of the numerical threat Aaron was looking at when he turned around on the curb by the courthouse.

As things progressed, the only real fact in dispute was the distance between the fired gun and the kid who was struck. Pat called Gary Pratt, the even tempered, experienced, and knowledgeable firearms examiner for the Syracuse Police Department. Pratt testified that the .25 was an operable firearm, still loaded when it was recovered. (Remember that the second count of the Indictment was Criminal Possession of a Weapon). He then identified the bullet, still intact, which had been recovered from the body of Roger Fields as a projectile fired from the same Titan semiautomatic. Given the established facts, it would have been pointless to challenge any of that (Although even back then the forensic identification of a projectile as one which was fired from a particular gun was starting to be called into question and today this kind of testimony is viewed cautiously. But given the fact that no one else was firing a gun in the vicinity, our pursuing such a challenge during trial would have been a waste of time and annoyed everybody). However, in identifying the weapon, Pratt did give us something to work with and it was something important to our side of the case:

> Normally this weapon is used for a close-in accuracy, within 45 feet or inwards. Beyond 45 feet the accuracy level starts deteriorating quite rapidly to a point where maybe 75 or 100 feet you may not even be able to hit a target the size of a human being.

Even the prosecution had to concede that Aaron was no closer to Fields than 50 feet when he fired (per the testimony of the evidence technician Knittle), so Pratt's testimony bolstered our claim of a random shot (thereby edging us away from the Murder count). To develop what Pratt had acknowledged, we called our own expert witness, John Pantaleo, the former head firearms examiner for the Sheriff's Department. He also, conveniently, was Gary Pratt's former boss, guru, and instructor. Pantaleo was a true marksman (winning several police pistol competitions) and during his career had conducted over 5,000 forensic examinations of guns. He test-fired the Titan used in this case at a controlled gun range. From 75 feet away and taking five shots, he was unable to even hit the paper target. In his expert opinion, this pistol had very poor accuracy and could only hit its intended target in at a range of 10 to 15 feet at most. There wasn't much that Pat could challenge him on on cross. He started out with trying to get Pantaleo to concede that sometimes even great athletes have a bad day and maybe that was the reason John missed the silhouette target five times at 75 feet. Pantaleo wasn't insulted; he just sort of stared Pat down. It was like asking Michael Jordan why he missed a 75-foot foul shot five times in a row.

When putting Pratt's testimony together with Pantaleo's (and they didn't conflict) I was hoping that any reasonable person would conclude that Aaron's firing the gun towards the oncoming crowd, with Roger Fields in the lead at least 50 feet away, was simply a tragic and unlucky random shot.

We were still left with the question of whether Aaron was the kind of person who could harbor a depraved indifference to human life.

I called his parents, Manny and Rose, not just to establish that Aaron was a good and respectful child who had never caused them or anyone else the least bit of trouble, but also to create a comfortable platform from which the jury could see that in most respects Aaron was an ordinary teenager, not unlike their own kids.

In what I'm sure he thought to be a magnanimous gesture intended to show what a fair-minded guy he was, P.J. allowed Manny and Rose to sit in on the trial during the prosecution's case. Ordinarily, witnesses who appear on either party's witness list are excluded from attending the trial (on the theory that they might tailor their testimony in response to hearing other witnesses). There are exceptions for expert witnesses or consultants, but on the whole most other witnesses are required to be sequestered until called unless the other party consents. To my mild surprise, Pat did not consent and I urged P.J. to allow them to stay in support of their 18 year old son; they were not witnesses to the shooting and were only going to testify to the character of their son. P.J. ruminated on this weighty issue ("I have mixed feelings on it") but finally allowed it. To me, it was a no-brainer and really shouldn't have been an issue in the first place.

I was reminded of an incident with one of P.J.'s former colleagues, Jim Anderson, a tall and very witty guy with a heavy Bronx accent. He was a well-liked City Court Judge who had unexpectedly passed away after serving as a newly elected County Court Judge for just a few months.

I was representing a sad but very sweet guy who had a serious substance abuse problem which led him to burglarize a workman's truck and steal the guy's tools and a gun. I wanted my client's family to sit in on the trial and the D.A. (for yet another hard to understand reason) wanted the family excluded. Anderson wasn't having any of that: "Ya know, Mr. D.A., they put a guy on trial two thousand years ago and they wouldn't let his friends or family sit in either. Ain't gonna happen here in my Court." Although his career was short-lived, Anderson had a special place in my Judicial Hall of Fame for two other reasons: he sent an operative gun with live ammunition into a deliberating jury in that same trial – the Court bailiff nearly had a heart attack –and he once told a defendant who wanted a guarantee that he wouldn't go to jail if he pleaded guilty that "Hey, mister, America is the land of opportunity, not guarantees."

In any case, Aaron's caring parents were able to sit quietly through the trial and it could not have escaped the jury's attention that they appeared to be decent people

Aaron Tells His Story

There was never any question, at least in my mind, that Aaron would testify in his own defense and explain what happened from his point of view. He was intelligent, good looking, quiet, and polite. Captain Walsh's initial assessment of him was right: he was not a gangbanger. More to the point, he was not a murderer and I was hopeful that the jury would see that.

Putting your client on the stand is a strategy that most lawyers loathe. Many refuse to do it at all even though it's ultimately really never up to them. It's the client's call, his absolute right, and you can do what you can to dissuade him from doing it but you can't stop him. Even if the guy intends to lie, and you know he intends to lie, you can't refuse to call him. (You can't help him lie but you are obliged to put him up there). I recall one of my adversaries facing this kind of dilemma when I was an Assistant D.A. and, to my delight, the thug I was prosecuting in a gun possession case decided to testify notwithstanding the fact that the proof against him was overwhelming. His lawyer didn't think this was a very good idea:

LAWYER: The defense calls Larry Williams.

LAWYER: You are Larry Williams, is that right?

DEFENDANT: Yeah, that's right.

LAWYER: And Mr. Williams, you are choosing to take the stand and testify in your own defense in this case, is that right?

DEFENDANT: Yeah, that's right.

LAWYER: And we discussed that even though you have a right to testify, you don't have to do this and in fact I advised you not to, isn't that right?

DEFENDANT: Yeah, that's right.

LAWYER: And despite what I told you . . . .

At this point, the Judge mercifully interceded:

THE COURT: Hey, just write the guy a letter, willya?

Every lawyer knows that the best defense is really no defense at all; the key to winning is keeping the jury focused on the thought that the prosecution hasn't proven its case and the less "proof" you put forward the better your chances. Once you start calling witnesses, or worse, once you put the client on the stand, you're inviting the jury to start thinking about which side did the "better" job, whose witnesses are more believable, who has the stronger proof. These are all the wrong questions. The question – the only question – is and always has to be has the prosecution proven its case beyond a reasonable doubt? If you keep the jury focused on that alone, you are ahead of the game.

Nevertheless, it was pretty much of a given that I would call Aaron. For one thing, this wasn't a whodunnit and the facts weren't much in dispute. The kid foolishly let two shots fly, thinking he would scare off his pursuers. That was the question: what were you thinking? Pretty difficult to get the jury to understand either self-defense or Aaron's lack of intention to harm anybody without calling him.

His testimony was not lengthy. I established his age, where, how, and why he acquired the gun – which he had never previously used and which he had bought for self-protection – and why he fired the shots at his pursuers. ("I just fired it in the direction of the crowd that was chasing me. . . I was scared they were going to hurt me and my brother and Neal.") He wore a shirt and tie and wire-rimmed glasses, looking like he was about to address a faculty meeting or a student assembly. I made it a point to have him tell the jury that he was on schedule to graduate on time but that had been interrupted by his arrest. He also reminded the jury that he could not see very well at a distance without his glasses and on the day of the shooting he didn't have them. It wasn't so much, really, that he had vital information that the jury hadn't heard before; it was more a matter of this young earnest-looking guy was willing to answer whatever questions the D.A. would challenge him with. On the whole, I think he did pretty well.

Pat's cross-examination was to the point and aggressive without being offensive or inappropriate. He smartly had Aaron hold and point the (unloaded) gun and asked him, repeatedly, what his intent was in firing it, forcing him to acknowledge he had an awareness of many people in the immediate vicinity. Pat occasionally went too far in his questioning; P.J. overruled every one of my objections, mechanically reciting that it was cross-examination as if that was an automatic license to ask virtually any question, whether relevant or preposterous. (This is not uncommon with many judges but P.J.'s lack of understanding of even the basic rules of evidence elevated stupidity into a near-art form.)

On the whole, I got what I wanted from Aaron's testimony: no stumbles, no attitudinal disruptions, and conveying the sense that this was a decent young guy who found himself in a dangerous situation which was made more dangerous by his lack of judgment, not any criminal intention.

"Ooh Eddie, ooh Eddie"

We could tell that the jury was paying close attention to the summations. Pat emphasized the number of people so recklessly endangered by the shooting. I emphasized the number of people so recklessly chasing Aaron and his brother and that he was the one who felt endangered.

By trial's end, I had persuaded (maybe even forced) P.J. to give a "justification" (self-defense) instruction. He clearly didn't want to, but he knew that we had laid a sufficient foundation for the instruction and he was mindful, as ever, that he could get reversed for failing to give it. What started out as a two-count Indictment (Murder and Criminal Possession of a Weapon Second Degree) had now become five counts for the jury to choose from (Murder, Manslaughter in the Second Degree, Criminally Negligent Homicide, Criminal Possession of a Weapon Second Degree and Criminal Possession of a Weapon Third Degree). It all turned on how the jury saw the circumstances and Aaron's intent.

Given the rambling and nearly incoherent instructions on the law P.J. gave the jury, we anticipated that the deliberations would be rocky and that they would come back with several questions for clarification. Joe and I decided to stick around in the courtroom instead of going back to our offices. It was a good thing that we did.

Although lawyers' eavesdropping next to the closed door of a jury room is strictly verboten, the court attendants who stand guard are invariably gossipy reporters of what at least they think is going on. And most of the time they are happy to share their "inside" knowledge. It's largely useless information, frequently wildly unreliable; but lawyers are desperate for even the vaguest hint of what might be happening inside the sanctum sanctorum of the jury room, so these court attendants receive inordinate attention, even if at the end of the day it's pointless.

The one thing that we did reliably learn was that there were an unusual number of raised voices and sometimes yelling behind the jury door. This surprised me, not because there were raised voices (not uncommon during deliberations), but because this jury consisted of mostly women. It had been my experience that female jurors want to discuss and examine (sometimes to the point of tediousness), not berate and yell (definitely a guy thing). We didn't know, of course, what they were yelling about, but after an hour and a half the answer came in the form of a note, one which we all immediately recognized as a harbinger of major danger.

The note materialized in the typical P.J. Cunningham fashion. Joe and I were standing around one of the courtroom counsel tables chatting with the court reporter when P.J. came flying out of his chambers door, his too big by half judicial robes billowing behind him. "Ooh, Eddie, ooh, Eddie. We got a problem here. We got a problem here.

They sent out a note. Go get Pat willya?"

The standard protocol – in fact the law – requires the note to be marked as a court exhibit, and after it's read the contents are supposed to be discussed by the lawyers and the judge so that an appropriate response can be fashioned. Sometimes it's as routine as a request to see a trial exhibit or a readback of a witness' testimony (on at least two occasions I actually had a jury request a readback of the entire trial). In P.J.'s courtroom, however, everything was a skewed adventure and very little followed standard protocol.

It took a few minutes, but we all assembled in P.J.'s chambers. He had the note in his hand and his size seven penny loafers were perched on the desk in front of him. He read the note out loud. "Judge, we are hopelessly deadlocked in the first count, Murder in the Second Degree. What should we do?" He peered over his bifocals and looked at me.

For Joe and me, this was welcome news, as it meant that it was likely that Aaron was going to escape a Murder conviction. For me, the response was a no-brainer. I say to P.J., "Well tell them to go to the Manslaughter count."

You will remember that Manslaughter in the Second Degree was the next lesser included offense, punishable by a max of 15 years, not life, a charge not in the original Indictment, and a charge that P.J. grudgingly included as an instruction in his final charge to the jury only after I hectored him to death about it.

Pat was sitting there silently, considering what the proper response for the People should be.

During this conversation, and unbeknownst to me, Judge Walter Gorman had been looming in the doorway behind me, listening to our back and forth. It wouldn't have surprised me at all if P.J. had called Gorman to help him resolve what for most judges would have been a routine problem, but for P.J. it was a real brain twister. Gorman was a tall, bald, ex-Marine, an experienced trial judge who thoroughly enjoyed his job and enjoyed lawyers in general. He couldn't stand rude lawyers and the former D.A., Dick Hennessy in particular, and he made no bones about it. (Hennessy wasn't rude; he was just a ballsy in your face guy and Gorman had an instinctive dislike of him, one Irishman to another.) He tolerated pretty much everybody else. He had a subdued sense of humor, and always had a bemused Irish twinkle in his eye, probably attributable to being the father of eight kids and owning a bulldog named Charlotte he was very fond of. Gorman knew that P.J. was a fool, but he was tolerant of him to the point of always trying to guide him in the right direction. Like now.

Seemingly out of nowhere, Gorman says, "You can't do that. You wouldn't be able to retry the guy for Murder."

I loved Gorman, but at that moment I mightily restrained myself from blurting out, "Who the fuck asked you?"

P.J. says, "Gee, you think so Walter?" and the two of them then glide off to a side discussion with Gorman teaching P.J. some pretty rudimentary lessons in criminal procedure and double jeopardy, lessons which I had been banking on P.J. remaining as ignorant of as ever.

While this was going on, I say to P.J., "Judge, can I see that note?"

It was as if I had just caught P.J. looking up the dress of the court reporter, and he hurriedly digs into his pants pocket under his robe to pull out the creased sheet of notebook paper bearing the jury's message.

"Oh, yeah Eddie, yeah, I was gonna show it to you. I was gonna show it to you."

Nobody bothered to comment or point out that P.J.'s pocket was an entirely inappropriate place to keep the note which, as I said earlier, was supposed to be marked for the record as a Court exhibit.

P.J. handed me the folded and now somewhat crumpled note, and Pat, Joe, and I moved over to the tall window on the north side of the room where there was better light. I placed the note on top of the radiator and unfolded it. It read as follows:

"Judge, we are hopelessly deadlocked in the first count, Murder in the Second Degree. What should we do? We are deadlocked at 11-1 for Not Guilty."

Pat quietly groaned. Joe's jaw dropped. I just smirked. Not reading the note in full to us was exactly what I would have expected this racist little judicial weasel to have done. Pat and I briefly exchanged looks. With little hesitation, and weary resignation in his voice, Pat said, "Oh for Chrissakes. Tell them to go to Man 2."

And that's what happened. With the prosecution consenting to Manslaughter in the Second Degree, P.J. really had no choice, despite his own theory that Aaron's recklessness was "an assassination".

So the jury was called back into the courtroom and P.J. told them that if they were unable to reach unanimity on the first count (Murder) they should go on to the second (Manslaughter). The reported numerical deadlock of 11-1 was not mentioned but it was pretty obvious to all of us that the "one", the holdout, was a sour-faced guy in the back row, a University professor wearing the requisite tweed jacket and

Timberland boots. Two of the women in the front row turned and looked over to him with we-told-you-so looks. The whole proceeding took less than five minutes and the jury once again retired to resume deliberations.

There's a list that I carry around in my head. It's not a long one. It's composed of things that I'd really like to have happen in my life but I know that they aren't going to. Like becoming six feet tall. I'm 76 years old and 5'9". I'm still working on it. Another item on my wish list is being able to sit in and listen to a jury deliberate one of the cases I've tried. For all the drama and mystery of the trial work I've done, what has gone on behind those closed doors has remained unknown and unknowable for me. The only knowledge I have ever had of these things are a few unsatisfying anecdotal snatches that some jurors have been kind enough to share. (Most jurors who are willing to talk to you tell you the same thing: you did a great job; it was a really interesting experience). So, what happened inside the Aaron Dempsey jury room after P.J. told them they should bypass the Murder count and deliberate on Manslaughter is only known to me by virtue of a few jurors being willing (in fact eager) to share it with me.

Here's what I now know happened:

The two women in the front row who had tried to stare down the hold-out professor were solid "Not Guilty" votes and fully accepted our argument of self-defense. They were joined by two other women who were inclined towards "compromise" (how do you "compromise" on the number of years an 18 year old has to spend in prison for an act of recklessness that was clearly his fault but took another kid's life?) and these four pretty much drove the argument. The remaining seven (but for the professor) were open to some kind of leniency. The professor wasn't budging. The group tried to ignore him for a while and the four women driving the deliberation proposed Criminally Negligent Homicide, something they instinctively felt was a lesser crime (they didn't know it at the time but Criminally Negligent Homicide carries a max of but four years; Manslaughter Second, the next step up, was punishable by fifteen). It was a no-sale for the professor, although he did concede that the D.A. hadn't proven Aaron's intent on the Weapons count. (They were unanimous on the lesser count of Criminal Possession of a Weapon Third).

Since the professor was not inclined to compromise, the group reached what they considered a fair result. They voted to convict Aaron of Manslaughter and then some of them would ask Judge Cunningham to extend leniency in sentencing him. Beyond the fact that such jury "recommendations" are meaningless under New York law, clearly this group didn't know who they were dealing with. One of the jurors who wanted to vote for an acquittal later told me, "We went along with a conviction because most of us felt that if it was a hung jury and the D.A. tried the case again Aaron would never get another jury as sympathetic as this one was." Which was probably true. What was also probably true was that P.J. Cunningham would preside yet again at any new trial.

So that's how it turned out. Aaron was convicted of Manslaughter and Criminal Possession of a Weapon Third.

The four female jurors who lobbied for leniency not only wrote a letter in support of Aaron but, quite remarkably, also showed up at his sentencing to advocate for leniency. And, of course, to almost no one's shock, P.J. ignored them and imposed the maximum sentence of 15 years.

It took almost a year of my life to work towards "justice" for Aaron and I'm still not sure we ever really got there. I was grateful for the compassion and wisdom of the jury. I was grateful too that, in the end, I outlasted P.J. I'm not sure it was justice or just plain karma, but a few years after Aaron's trial, P.J.'s remark about Dominicans being great baseball players but too many of them were drug dealers found its way back to the Commission on Judicial Conduct; by then they had had their fill of P.J. Cunningham. It pretty much did it for him. Facing certain removal, he resigned shortly afterward.

ABOUT THE AUTHOR

Ed Menkin is a criminal defense lawyer in Syracuse, New York. A proud son of the Bronx with a Ph.D. in Shakespeare, he has hiked across the Grand Canyon and ridden a hot air balloon over the Serengeti Plains at dawn. But his greatest adventures, and his most fun, have taken place in Court and these are some of his stories.

This is his second book, a continuation of reminiscences of his experience of over 40 years as a lawyer working for justice.

His first book, "Death on the Doorstep", is available on Amazon:

http://amzn.com/1079316817

For more information about Ed, please visit his website:

http://www.edmenkin.com/

Made in the USA
Columbia, SC
10 March 2021